Teach Yourself Data Analytics in 30 Days

Learn to use Python and Jupyter Notebooks by exploring fun, real-world data projects

David Clinton

Teach Yourself Data Analytics in 30 Days

Learn to use Python and Jupyter Notebooks by exploring fun, real-world data projects

David Clinton

ISBN 978-1-7777210-0-8

Bootstrap IT (a project of DBC Technology Services Inc.) provides books, courses, and articles covering cloud, Linux, IT security, and data management skills.

Contents

Getting Started with Data Analytics and Python . . . **1**
- Programming with Python . . . 1
- Installing Python . . . 2
- Virtual Python environments . . . 3
- Working with Python modules . . . 4
- Using Jupyter Notebooks . . . 4
- Installing Jupyter Notebooks . . . 6
- Storing and protecting data . . . 7
- Getting help . . . 7

Comparing Wages With Consumer Price Index Data **11**
- Working With the API . . . 12
- Working with CPI and salary data . . . 14
- Merge and plot our dataframes . . . 23

Wages and CPI: Reality Check . . . **27**
- Confirm the integrity of your data . . . 27
- Establish a historical context for your data . . . 30
- Incorporate S&P 500 quotes . . . 32
- Warning: Gotchas ahead! . . . 33
- Calculate rate of increase for both CPI and S&P . . 39

Working With Major US Storm Data . . . **43**
- What Is a Major Storm? . . . 43

Where Does Major Storm Data Come From? 44
What Does the Historical Record Show? 45
US Hurricane Data: 1851-2019 46
US Tropical Storm Data: 1851-1965, 1983-2019 . . . 56

Property Rights and Economic Development 69
How Do You Measure Conditions and Outcomes? . 69
Getting the Data 71
Visualizing Data Sets Using Scatter Plots 75
Adding "Hover" Visibility 77
Adding a Regression Line 78
Other Considerations 81

How Representative Is Your Government? 83
Scraping data from a single vote 86
Automating vote tabulation 88
What did we learn? 93
Could government be more representative? 95

Does Wealth Influence the Prevalence of Mental Illness? 97
My assumptions 99
Plotting the data 101
Thinking about our data 104

Do Birthdays Make Elite Athletes? 107
Where Does the NHL Hide Its Data? 108
How to Use Python to Scrape NHL Statistics 109
How to Visualize the Raw Data 111
What Do Histograms Really Tell Us? 113
Make Sure to Use the Right Tools For the Job 115

Do Gun Control Laws Impact Gun Violence? 117
Quantifying International Gun Laws 118

Importing Gun Violence Data 122
Plotting International Gun Violence Data 123
US Gun Laws and Gun Violence 126
What's next? 130

Getting Started with Data Analytics and Python

This curriculum won't turn you into a data scientist in the formal sense of the word: don't think 30 days is enough to compete with a Ph.D in statistics. But what this curriculum *will* do is teach you how to use Python and Jupyter Notebooks to find, process, manage, and interpret a wide range of data sources.

Is that enough for you? Do you *need* to become a data scientist? My guess is that you probably wouldn't be here if that was what you were really after. But whatever you do now, you can probably do it better with some basic analytics tools. And have much more fun while you're at it.

So why not quit talking about it and get good and started already?

Programming with Python

This curriculum assumes you've got at least a very basic understanding of programming in general and Python programming in particular. If you feel you're not quite there yet, catching up shouldn't take you too long.

Feel free to check out these valuable resources:

- Python For Beginners an official "getting started" page[1] with links to loads of great tools.
- Learn Python Programming[2] is a set of quick and to-the-point tutorials.
- Get into Python[3] is a hands-on tutorial that lets you run the code you're learning right in your browser.

Installing Python

The good news is that most operating systems come with Python pre-installed. Not sure your particular OS got the memo? Open a command prompt/terminal and type: `python --version` (or `python3 --version`).

If Python's installed, you'll probably see something like this:

```
$ python --version
Python 3.7.6
```

or this:

```
$ python3 --version
Python 3.8.5
```

At this point, by the way, the version number you get had better not begin with a `2` (as in `2.7`) - that's no longer supported and using such an old release will add some serious vulnerabilities to your software.

If you do need to install Python manually, you're best off using Python's official documentation (python.org/downloads)[4] - that'll be the most complete and up-to-date source available.

[1]https://www.python.org/about/gettingstarted/
[2]https://pythonbasics.org/
[3]https://jobtensor.com/Tutorial/Python/en/Introduction
[4]https://www.python.org/downloads/

Virtual Python environments

It's important to note that not all Python versions - even those from 3.x - will necessarily behave quite the way you expect. You may, for instance, find that you need a library written for version 3.9, but that there's no way to get it working on your 3.7 system.

Upgrading your system version to 3.9 *might* work out well for you, but it could also cause some unexpected and unpleasant consequences. It's hard to predict when a particular Python library may also be holding up bits of the OS. Pull the original version of the library and you might end up disabling the OS itself. Don't laugh: I've done it to myself.

The solution is to run Python for your project within a special virtual environment that's isolated from your larger OS. That way, you can install all the libraries and versions you like without having to worry about damaging your work system. You can do this using a full-scale virtual container running a Docker or (as I prefer) LXD image, or on a standalone AWS cloud instance. But you can also use Python's own `venv` module. That can be as simple as running this single command:

```
python3 -m venv /path/to/new/virtual/environment
```

You'll want to read the official documentation (docs.python.org/3/library/venv.html)[5] for the virtual environment instructions specific to your host OS.

[5]https://docs.python.org/3/library/venv.html

Working with Python modules

Not all Python functionality will be available out of the box. Sometimes you'll need to tell Python to load a particular module through a declaration within your code:

```
import pandas as pd
```

But some modules will need to be installed manually from the host command line before they can even be imported. For such cases, Python recommends their installer program, `pip` or, in some cases, the `conda` tool from the anaconda distribution.

```
pip3 install pandas matplotlib plotly
```

You can read more about using pip for the proper care and feeding of your Python system here: docs.python.org/3/installing[6].

All the software you'll need to run the projects in this book should be noted where appropriate. But do pay attention to any unexpected error messages you might encounter in case your environment is somehow missing something.

Using Jupyter Notebooks

Once upon a time the lines of code you'd write to pull off the analytics we're after would find themselves all snuggled up together in a single text file whose name ended with a `.py` suffix. When you wanted to run your code to see how things

[6]https://docs.python.org/3/installing/index.html

went, you'd do it from the command line (or a powerful and complicated source-code editor like Visual Studio Code).

Fun. But it meant that, for *anything* to work, it *all* had to work. That would make it harder to troubleshoot when something didn't go according to spec. But it would also make it a lot harder to play around with specific details just to see what happens - which is where a lot of our most innovative ideas come from. And it also made it tough to share live versions of our code across the internet.

Jupyter Notebooks are JSON-based files (using .ipynb extensions) that, along with their various hosting environments, have gone a long way to solving all those problems. Notebooks move the processing environment for just about any data-oriented programming code using Python (or other languages) from your workstation to your web browser.

For me, a notebook's most powerful feature is the way you can run subsets of your code within individual cells. This makes it easy to break down long and complex programs into easily readable - and executable - snippets. Whatever values were created will remain in the kernel memory until output for a particular cell or for the entire kernel are cleared.

This lets you re-run previous or subsequent cells to see what impact a change might have. It also means resetting your environment for a complete start-over is as easy as selecting `Restart Kernel and Clear All Outputs`.

You can install Jupyter Notebooks locally on your Python-enabled host and run it from within your browser. Alternatively, you can run notebooks on third-party hosting services like Google's Colaboratory or - for a cost - cloud providers like Amazon's SageMaker Studio Notebooks and Microsoft's Azure Notebook.

If you do decide to make an old sysadmin happy and host your own notebooks, you'll need to choose between classic notebooks and the newer JupyterLab. Both run nicely within your browser, but JupyterLab comes with more extensions and lets you work with multiple notebook files (and terminal access) within a single browser tab.

JupyterHub, just to be complete, is a server version built to provide authenticated notebook access to multiple users. You can serve up to 100 or so users from a single cloud server using The Littlest JupyterHub (tljh.jupyter.org)[7]. For larger deployments involving clusters of servers, you'd probably be better off with a Kubernetes version known as Zero to JupyterHub with Kubernetes[8].

Installing Jupyter Notebooks

Whichever version you choose, if you decide to install locally, the Jupyter project officially recommends doing it through the Python Anaconda distribution and its binary package manager, Conda. Various guides to doing that are available for various OS hosts. But this official page jupyterlab.io/install[9] is a good place to start.

At some point you'll probably run into trouble. With JupyterLabs in particular, extensions can be a bit fiddly when installing. It's useful therefore to be aware of the `labextension` tool. These simple commands illustrate how the tool can work.

[7]https://tljh.jupyter.org/en/latest/
[8]https://zero-to-jupyterhub.readthedocs.io/en/latest/
[9]http://jupyterlab.io/install.html

```
jupyter labextension list
jupyter labextension install jupyterlab-plotly
jupyter labextension install plotlywidget
```

And always watch closely for error messages that can tell you important things about your environment.

Storing and protecting data

Please spare a few thoughts for your poor, unappreciated data. By which I mean the CSV or JSON files you might have generated while collecting and cleaning data sets. But I also mean your actual `.ipynb` notebook files. Remember: it's true that Jupyter will regularly auto save your notebooks. But where does that saved file actually live? Wherever you left it on the host - which might be as ephemeral as a Docker container.

What happens when that host is shut down for the last time and decommissioned (or corrupted beyond repair)? Your CSV and `.ipynb` files go with it. What can you do to preserve all that data? Make sure up-to-date copies exist in reliable places.

After all, data doesn't back itself up.

Getting help

The internet is host to more knowledge than any one human being could possibly remember, or even organize. More often than not, we use search to access the tiny fragments of that knowledge that we need at a given time. Effective search, however, is far more than just typing a few related words into the search field and hitting Enter. There's method to the madness. Here are some powerful tips that will work on any major search engine. My own favorite is DuckDuckGo.

Use your problem to find a solution

Considering that countless thousands of people have worked with the same technology you're now learning, the odds are very high that at least some of them have run into the same problem you did. And at least a few of those will have posted their questions to an online user forum like Stack Overflow. The quickest way to get at look at the answers they received is to search using the exact language that you encountered.

Did your problem generate an error message? Paste exactly that text into your search engine. Were there any log messages? Find and post those, too.

Be precise

The internet has billions of pages, so vague search results are bound to include a whole lot of false positives. That's why you want to be as precise as possible. One powerful trick is to enclose your error message in quotation marks, telling the search engine that you're looking for an exact phrase, rather than a single result containing all or most of the words somewhere on the page. However, you don't want to be so specific that you end up narrowing your results down to zero.

Therefore, for an entry from the Apache error log like this:

```
[Dec 16 02:15:44 2020] [error] [client 54.211.9.96]\
 Client sent malformed Host header
```

...you should leave out the date and client IP address, because there's no way anyone else got those exact details. Instead, include only the "Client sent..." part in quotations:

```
"Client sent malformed Host header"
```

If that's still too broad, consider adding the strings `Apache` and `[error]` outside the quotation marks.

Search engines let you narrow down your search by time. If your problem is specific to a relatively recent release version, restrict your search to just the last week or month.

Sometimes an outside search engine will do a better job searching through a large web site than the site's own internal tool (I'm looking at you: Government of Canada). If you feel the solution to your problem is likely to be somewhere on a particular site - like Stack Overflow's admin cousin, Server Fault - but you can't find it yourself, you can restrict results to just that one site:

```
"gss_accept_sec_context(2) failed:" site:serverfaul\
t.com
```

Finally, if you see that many or all of the false positives you're getting seem to include a single word that is very unlikely to occur in the pages you're looking for, exclude it with a dash. In this example you, of course, were looking for help learning how to write Bash scripts, but you kept seeing links with advice for aspiring Hollywood screenwriters. Here's how to solve it:

```
writing scripts -movie
```

Good luck!

David Clinton[10]

The Data Project[11]

---

[10]https://bootstrap-it.com/davidclinton/
[11]https://thedataproject.net

Comparing Wages With Consumer Price Index Data

How many people do you know who have a favorite US government department? I've got a favorite, and I'm not even American. It's the Bureau of Labor Statistics, and I've been enjoying the torrents of employment and economics-related data they produce for decades, now.

But my admiration for BLS jumped to a new level when I discovered their well-supported application programming interface (API). This opens up all that delicious data to smart retrieval through our Python scripts. And it gives us some rich resources for discovery.

Let me illustrate with a relatively simple example. I'm going to use the API to request US consumer price index (CPI) and wage and salary statistics between 2002 and 2020.

The CPI is a measure of the price of a basket of essential consumer goods. It's an important proxy for changes in the cost of living which, in turn, is an indicator of the general health of the economy.

Our wages data will come from the BLS Employment Cost Index covering "wages and salaries for private industry workers in all industries and occupations." A growing employment index would, at first glance, suggest that things are getting better for most people.

However, seeing the average employment wages trends in isolation isn't all that useful. After all, the highest salary won't do you much good if your basic expenses are higher still. I know what I'm talking about here, since I grew up in the 1970s. Back then, high inflation would often completely cancel out the value of a raise at work. (Although I can't say I remember that having too much of an impact on my brief career as a before-school newspaper carrier earning $10-15 a week.)

So the goal is to pull both the CPI and wages data sets and then correlate them. This will show us how wages have been changing *in relation to* costs.

Working With the API

There are two and a half things you'll need to successfully access the API:

- BLS endpoint addresses matching the specific data series you need
- Python code to launch the request
- (In case you'll need them) A BLS API key to unlock higher request rates

Getting the series endpoint addresses you need may take some digging around in the BLS website. However, the most popular data sets are accessible through a single page.[12] The following image shows you what that looks like, including the endpoint codes - like "LNS11000000" for the Civilian Labor Force set.

[12]https://data.bls.gov/cgi-bin/surveymost?bls

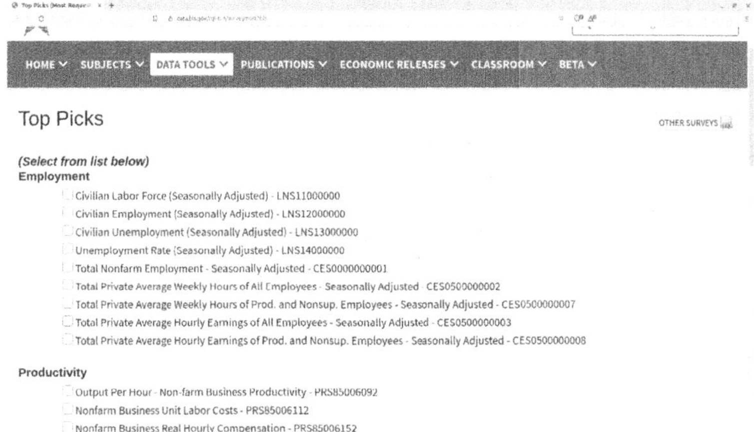

You can also search for data sets on this page[13]. Searching for "computer," for instance, will take you to a list that includes the deeply tempting "Average hourly wage for level 11 computer and mathematical occupations in Austin-Round Rock, TX." The information you'll discover by expanding that selection will include its series ID (endpoint) of "WMU00124201020000001500000011"

Because I know you can barely contain your curiosity, I'll tell you that it turns out that level 11 computer and mathematical professionals in Austin-Round Rock, Texas could expect to earn $51.76/hour in 2019.

How do you turn series IDs into Python-friendly data? Well that's what we'll learn next.

Getting the GET and PUT requests exactly right can be complicated. But because I enjoy a simple life, I decided to go with one of the available third-party Python libraries. The one I use is called, simply, `bls` and is available through Oliver Sherouse's GitHub repo[14]. You install the library on your host

[13]https://beta.bls.gov/dataQuery/search
[14]https://github.com/OliverSherouse/bls

machine using:

```
pip install bls
```

While you're at the command line, you might as well activate your BLS API key. You register for the API from this page[15]. They'll send you an email with your key and a validation URL that you'll need to click.

Once you've got your key, you export it to your system environment. On Linux or macOS, that would mean running something like this (where your key is substituted for the invalid one I used):

```
export BLS_API_KEY=lk88af0f0d5fd1iw290s52a01b8q
```

Working with CPI and salary data

With that out of the way, we're all set to start digging for CPI and employment gold. Importing these four libraries - including `bls` - will give us the tools we're going to need:

```
import pandas as pd
import matplotlib as plt
import numpy as np
import bls
```

Now I pass the BLS endpoint for the wages and salaries data series to the `bls.get_series` command from the `bls` library. I copied the endpoint from the popular data sets page on the BLS website. I'll assign the data series that comes back to the variable `wages` and then take a look at a sample from the data set.

[15] https://data.bls.gov/registrationEngine/

```
wages = bls.get_series('CIU2020000000000A')
wages
0          2002Q1          3.5
1          2002Q2          3.6
2          2002Q3          3.1
3          2002Q4          2.6
4          2003Q1          2.9
```

Assessing our two data series

For now, just note how the format of the first column of data consists of a year (2002, 2003, etc.) followed by the financial quarter (Q1, Q2, etc.) and the fact that the second column (3.5, 3.6) consists of percentages. We'll get back to that data set later. But right now we'll switch over to the CPI series.

We'll pull the CPI data series as the variable, `cpi`. I'll export the data to a CSV file named `cpi_data.csv` so it'll be available to me even if I accidentally overwrite the variable. I also happen to find it a bit easier to work with CSV files.

At any rate, I'll then read the CSV into a dataframe called `cpi_data` and do a bit of formatting by adding two column headers (`Date` and `CPI`).

```
cpi = bls.get_series('CUUR0000SA0')
cpi.to_csv('cpi_data.csv')
cpi_data = pd.read_csv('cpi_data.csv')
cpi_data.columns = 'Date','CPI'
```

Here's what my data will look like:

```
cpi_data
        Date        CPI
0        2002-01        177.100
1        2002-02        177.800
2        2002-03        178.800
3        2002-04        179.800
4        2002-05        179.800
...        ...        ...
222        2020-07        259.101
223        2020-08        259.918
224        2020-09        260.280
225        2020-10        260.388
226        2020-11        260.229
227 rows × 2 columns
```

If we want to correlate this CPI data with the wages series, the logical approach is to compare changes in both data sets as they occurred through time. But before that can happen, we'll need to overcome two serious problems:

- The CPI data is monthly while the wages data is quarterly (i.e., four increments per year). And the Date column in the CPI set is formatted differently (2002-01) than that of the wages set (2002Q1). Python won't know how to compare those columns as they currently exist.
- The CPI values are measured in points (177.10, etc.) while the wage changes are presented as percentages (3.5, etc). Those, too, won't be comparable in any useful way unless we clean things up a bit.

Manipulating the CPI data series

Python is built to be helpful in fixing those problems. Sure, I could always open up the data in CSV files and manually edit each row. But that would be boring and time consuming for the hundreds of rows we're working with. And it would be impossible for the millions of rows of data used by many other analytics projects.

So we're going to automate our data clean up.

We'll focus first on the CPI series. I'm going to use the Python `str.replace` method to search for any occurrence of `-03` (i.e., "March") in the `Date` column, and replace it with the string `Q1`. This will match the `Q1` records in my wages data set. I'll then do the same for the June, September, and December rows.

```
cpi_data['Date'] = cpi_data['Date'].str.replace('-0\
3', 'Q1')
cpi_data['Date'] = cpi_data['Date'].str.replace('-0\
6', 'Q2')
cpi_data['Date'] = cpi_data['Date'].str.replace('-0\
9', 'Q3')
cpi_data['Date'] = cpi_data['Date'].str.replace('-1\
2', 'Q4')
```

I'm sure there's syntax that would allow me to do all that in one line, but the couple of seconds it took me to copy and paste those lines hardly compared to the time it would have taken me to figure out the "more efficient" alternative. If automation threatens to take me longer than the manual way, then I vote for manual every time.

We can print out some data to show us what we've got so far:

```
cpi_data['Date']

0        2002-01
1        2002-02
2         2002Q1
3        2002-04
4        2002-05
          ...
222      2020-07
223      2020-08
224       2020Q3
225      2020-10
226      2020-11
Name: Date, Length: 227, dtype: object
```

The quarterly records are exactly the way we want them, but the rest are obviously still a problem. We should look for a characteristic that's unique to all the records we *don't* want to keep and use that as a filter. Our best (and perhaps only) choice is the dash ("-"). The `str.contains` method when set to `False` will, when run against the `Date` column as it is here, drop all the contents of all rows that contain a dash.

```
newcpi_data = cpi_data[(cpi_data.Date.str.contains(\
"-") == False)]
```

You'll want to confirm everything went as planned by printing a sample of your data. Everything here looks great. Note how there are now only 75 rows of data, as opposed to the 227 we began with.

```
newcpi
```

```
        Date        CPI
2        2002Q1        178.800
5        2002Q2        179.900
8        2002Q3        181.000
11        2002Q4        180.900
14        2003Q1        184.200
...        ...        ...
212        2019Q3        256.759
215        2019Q4        256.974
218        2020Q1        258.115
221        2020Q2        257.797
224        2020Q3        260.280
75 rows × 2 columns
```

If you like, you can save the data series in its final state to a CSV file:

```
newcpi_data.to_csv('cpi-clean.csv')
```

Converting percentages to "CPI" values

Well that's our formatting problem out of the way: we've converted the CPI data to quarterly increments and cleaned up the date format to match the wages data. Now we'll need to address the inconsistency between the absolute point values in the CPI set and the percentages that came with the wages data.

First, lets go get that data. Technically, if you've been following along on your own, you'll already have pulled the series back near the beginning, but it can't hurt to run it again.

Once again, I'll save the data to a CSV file (which, again, isn't necessary), push it to a dataframe I'll call `df`, and give it column headers. Naming the date column `Date` to match the CPI set will make things easier.

```
wages = bls.get_series('CIU2020000000000A')
wages.to_csv('bls_data_csv')
df = pd.read_csv('bls_wages_data_csv')
df.columns = 'Date','Wages'
```

The sample data we print looks just fine:

```
df.head()
        Date        Wages
0        2002Q1         3.5
1        2002Q2         3.6
2        2002Q3         3.1
3        2002Q4         2.6
4        2003Q1         2.9

newdf = df
```

Now, I should warn you that there's going to be some Fake Math(tm) here.

What's going on? Each of the percentages in the wages data series represents an annual average. So when we're told that the rate for the first quarter of 2002 was 3.5%, that means that if wages continued to rise at the current (first quarter) rate for a full 12 months, the annual average growth would have been 3.5%. But not 14%.

Which means the numbers we're going to work with will have to be adjusted. That's because the *actual* growth during, say, the three months of 2002 Q1 wasn't 3.5%, but only one quarter of that (or 0.875%). If I don't make this adjustment, but continue to map quarterly growth numbers to quarterly CPI prices, then our calculated output will lead us to think that wages are growing so fast that they've become detached from reality.

And here's where part of the fake math is going to rear its ugly head. I'm going to divide each quarterly growth rate by four. Or, in other words, I'll pretend that the *real* changes to wages during those three months were exactly one quarter of the reported year-over-year rate. But I'm sure that's almost certainly not true and is a gross simplification. However, for the big historical picture I'm trying to draw here, it's probably close enough.

Now that will still leave us with a number that's a percentage. But the corresponding CPI number we're comparing it to is, again, a point figure. To "solve" this problem I'll apply one more piece of fakery.

To convert those percentages to match the CPI values, I'm going to create a function. I'll feed the function the starting (2002 Q1) CPI value of 177.10. That'll be my baseline. I'll give that variable the name `newnum`.

For each iteration the function will make through the rows of my wages data series, I'll divide the current wage value (`x`) by 400. 100 simply converts the percentage (3.5, etc.) to a decimal (0.035). And the four will reduce the annual rate (12 months) to a quarterly rate (3 months).

To convert that to a usable number, I'll multiply it by the current value of `newnum` and then add `newnum` to the product. That should give us an approximation of the original CPI value adjusted by the related wage-growth percentage.

But, of course, this won't be a number that has any direct equivalent in the real world. Instead, it is, as I said, an arbitrary approximation of what that number might have been. But, again, I think it'll be close enough for our purposes.

Take a couple of minutes and read through the function. `global newnum` declares the variable as global. This makes it possible for me to replace the original value of `newnum` with the function's output so the percentage in the next row will be adjusted by the updated value. Note also how any strings (`str`) will be ignored. And, finally, note how the updated data series will populate the `newwages_data` variable.

```
newnum = 177.1
def process_wages(x):
    global newnum
    if type(x) is str:
        return x
    elif x:
        newnum = (x / 400) * newnum + newnum
        return newnum
    else:
        return
newwages = newdf.applymap(process_wages)
```

Let's check that new data:

```
newwages
```

	Date	Wages
0	2002Q1	178.649625
1	2002Q2	180.257472
2	2002Q3	181.654467
3	2002Q4	182.835221
4	2003Q1	184.160776
...	...	...
70	2019Q3	273.092663
71	2019Q4	275.140858
72	2020Q1	277.410770
73	2020Q2	279.421999
74	2020Q3	281.308097

75 rows × 2 columns

Looks great.

Merge and plot our dataframes

What's left? We need to merge our two data series. But since we've already done all the cleaning up and manipulation, this will go smoothly. I'll create a new dataframe called `merged_data` and feed it with the output of this `pd.merge` function. I simply supply the names of my two dataframes, and specify that the `Date` column should be the index.

```
merged_data = pd.merge(newcpi_data, newwages_data, \
on='Date')
```

Fast and friendly. No trouble at all. Go ahead and take a look:

```
merged_data
        Date        CPI              Wages
0        2002Q1        178.800        178.649625
1        2002Q2        179.900        180.257472
2        2002Q3        181.000        181.654467
3        2002Q4        180.900        182.835221
4        2003Q1        184.200        184.160776
...        ...        ...        ...
70        2019Q3        256.759        273.092663
71        2019Q4        256.974        275.140858
72        2020Q1        258.115        277.410770
73        2020Q2        257.797        279.421999
74        2020Q3        260.280        281.308097
75 rows × 3 columns
```

Our data is all there. We could visually scan through the CPI and Wages columns and look for any unusual relationships, but we didn't come this far to just look at numbers. Let's plot the thing.

Here we'll tell `plot` to take our merged dataframe (`merged_data`) and create a bar chart. Because there's an awful lot of data here, I'll extend the size of the chart with a manual `figsize` value. I set the x-axis labels to use values in `Date` column and, again because there are so many of them, I'll rotate the labels by 45 degrees to make them more readable. Finally, I'll set the label for the y-axis.

```
ax = merged_data.plot(kind='bar', figsize=(20, 7))
ax.set_xticklabels(merged_data.Date, rotation=45)
ax.set_ylabel('CPI vs. Wages and salaries - 12-mont\
h change')
ax.set_xlabel('Dates')
```

And this is what I got:

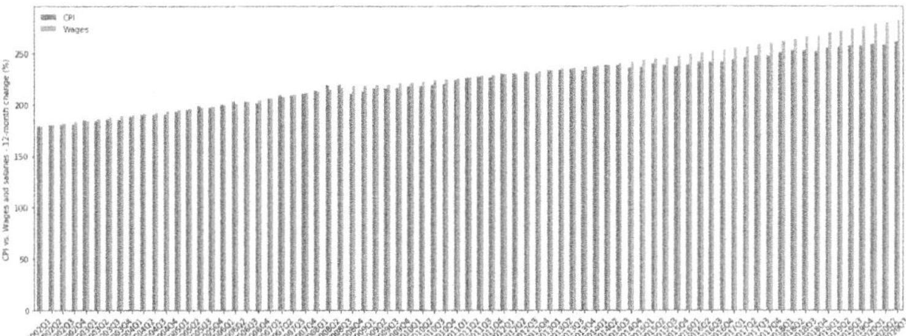

Because of the crowding, it's not especially easy to read. But you can see that the orange "Wages" bars are, for the most part, higher than the blue "CPI" bars. We'll have a stab at analyzing some of this in the next chapter.

Is there an easier way to display all this data? You bet there is. I can change the value of `kind` from `bar` to `line` and things will instantly improve. Here's how the new code will work as a line plot and with a grid:

```
ax = merged_data.plot(kind='line', figsize=(20, 7))
ax.set_ylabel('CPI vs. Wages and salaries - 12-mont\
h change')
ax.set_xlabel('Dates')
ax.grid()
```

And here's our new chart:

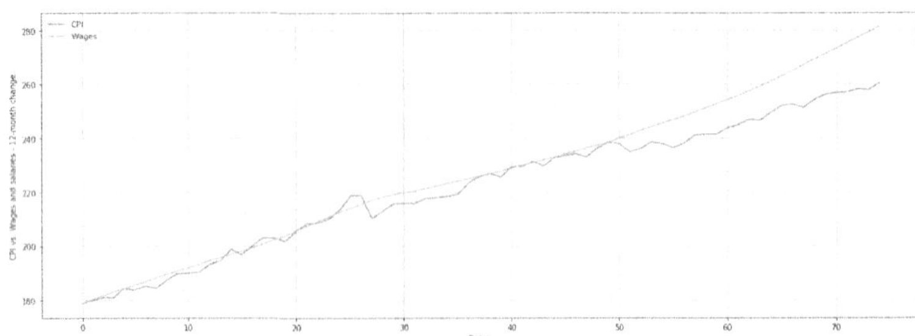

In the next chapter, we'll try to better understand the data we're using and then add historical S&P 500 index data as another metric.

Wages and CPI: Reality Check

We're supposed to be doing data *analytics* here, so just staring at pretty graphs probably isn't the whole point.

The CPI and wages data sets we plotted in the previous chapter, for instance, showed us a clear general correlation, but there were some visually recognizable anomalies. Unless we can connect those anomalies with historical events - and explain them in a historical context - we won't be getting the full value from our data.

Confirm the integrity of your data

But even before going there, we should confirm that our plots actually make sense in the context of their data sources. Working with our BLS examples, let's look at graphs to compare CPI and wages data from both before and after our manipulation. That way we can be sure that our math (and particularly our *fake* math) didn't skew things too badly.

Here's what our CPI data looked like when plotted using the raw data:

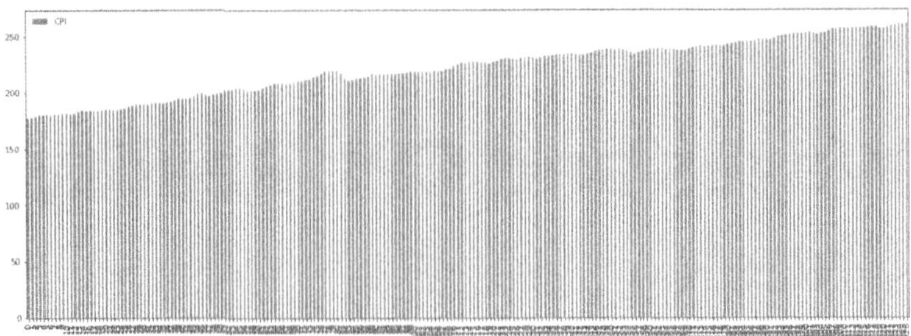

It's certainly a busy graph, but you can clearly see the gentle upward slope, punctuated by a handful of sudden jumps. Next. we'll see that same data after removing three out of every four months' data points. The same ups and downs are still visible. Given our overall goals, I'd categorize our transformation as a success.

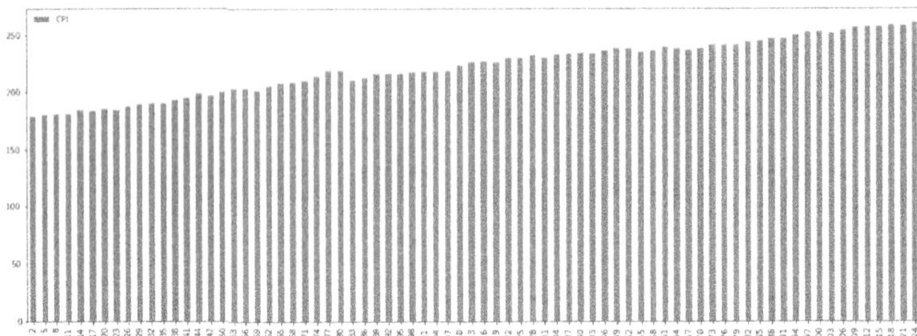

Now, how about the wages data? Here, because we moved from percentages to currency, the transformation was more intrusive and the risks of misrepresentation were greater. We'll also need to take into account the way a percentage will display differently from an absolute value. Here's the original data:

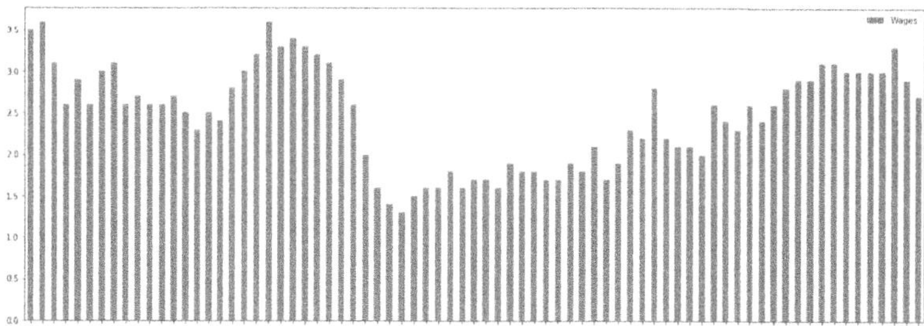

Note how there's no consistent curve - either upwards or downwards. That's because we're measuring the *rate* of growth as it took place within each individual quarter, not the growth itself. Now compare that with this line graph of that wage data, now converted to currency-based values:

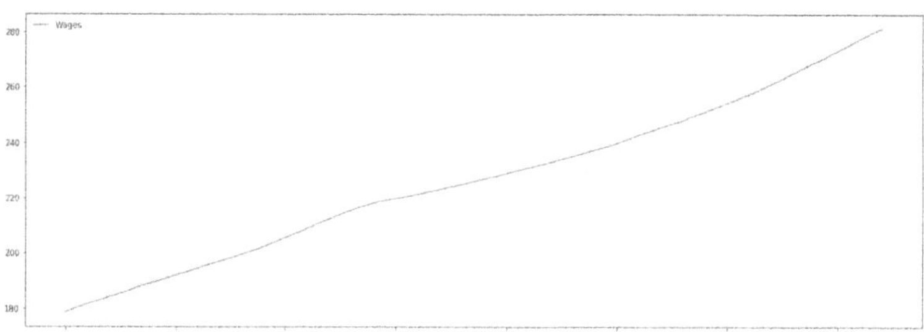

The gentle curve you see does make sense - it's about real growth, after all, not growth rates. But it's also possible to recognize a few spots where the curve steepens, and others where it smooths out. But why are the slopes so smooth in comparison with the percentage-based data? Look at the Y-axis labels: the index graph is measured in points between 180 and 280, while the percentage graph goes from 0-3.5. It's the *scale* that's different.

All in all, I believe we're safe concluding that what we've produced is a good match with our source data.

Establish a historical context for your data

Now let's look at those anomalies. Here, to refresh your memory, is our final line graph:

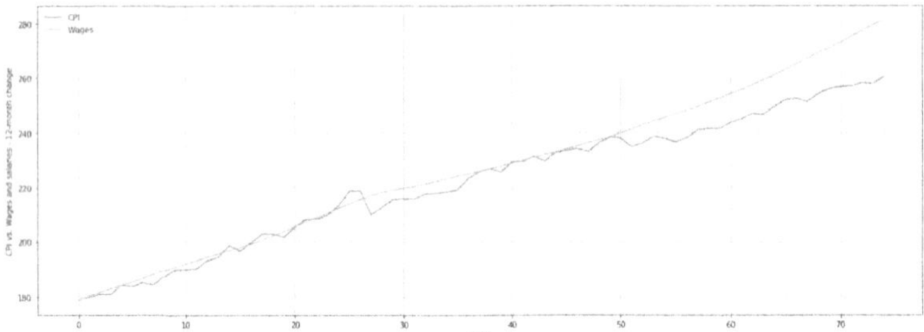

The most obvious point of interest is the accelerated wages growth starting some time in 2015 and noticeably picking up speed in 2017. This latter shift would seem to validate the claims that the Trump economy markedly improved the lives of workers. This would appear to be especially true considering how much faster wages rose over consumer costs, meaning that the pay raises made a real difference.

Of course, as can never be repeated enough, correlation is not the same as causation. It's possible that those changes had little or nothing to do with government actions. But, by the same token, we can't rule it out either. There's certainly an argument to be made that easing regulatory overhead and reducing the corporate tax rate are healthy policy changes that can stimulate business activity and, by extension, hiring.

Ok. Back to the graph. What was behind that huge spike in CPI back in 2008? Well, the famous Great Recession is always associated with 2008, isn't it?

The problem is that the subprime mortgage crisis that's blamed for the disaster only kicked in in the summer of that year. Our data shows significant increases in the *first* two quarters. And anyway, why would an economic downturn cause price increases? You'd think a recession would spark a drop in consumer demand which, in turn, should lead to a drop in prices.

I'm going to take full advantage of my ignorance of the actual facts and venture a wild guess. If I'm wrong, I'm sure someone reading this will correct me. The subprime economy was fed by artificially low lending rates and too much access to easy capital. Those conditions drew millions of Americans into the housing markets, fueled by flaky mortgages.

Now, a hot housing market should always lead to higher house prices (a simple product of the law of supply and demand). And housing prices make up around 33% of the CPI basket. Perhaps home prices were still rising into the final months before the market was hit with the full force of the meltdown.

I'm not sure this nails the whole backstory, but I do see some supporting evidence. Pulling the BLS "Housing in U.S. city average" cost index will allow us at least a glimpse behind the curtain.

```
housing = bls.get_series('SUUR0000SAH')
housing.to_csv('housing_index.csv')
```

If you look through the numbers for the years 2004-2007, you'll see the index only rose around 2.5 points between January and July. But between January, 2008 and July, 2008, it jumped more than four points before dropping off and remaining stagnant for the next six months. Perhaps that accounts for the spike.

```
Date                 Index
2004-01          112.5
2004-07          115.0

2005-01          115.6
2005-07          118.1

2006-01          119.6
2006-07          122.0

2007-01          122.767
2007-07          125.416

2008-01          125.966
2008-07          130.131
2008-08          129.985
2008-09          129.584
2008-10          129.189
2008-11          128.667
2008-12          128.495
```

The bottom line: if you were working in the US through those twenty years and you didn't enjoy regular pay raises, it's either your employer's fault or, if you were self-employed, yours. But don't blame the economy.

Incorporate S&P 500 quotes

Let's add one more data source to our mix. We've already seen how the CPI and employment wages trended over the past twenty years. Perhaps it would also be helpful to compare those numbers to a major US stock market index. Specifically, I'm going to import historical quotes from the Standard and Poors (S&P) 500 index.

The S&P 500 is a measure of the performance of 500 of the largest companies currently trading on major US stock exchanges. The index doesn't directly represent any real-world equities and has no direct value on its own. Instead, it's designed as a useful indicator of the health of the market as a whole.

If you're looking for a single number that neatly and reliably summarizes the state of the global equity investment environment over time, the S&P 500 is probably your best bet.

There are all kinds of ways to get the data we're after. I downloaded it from the Wall Street Journal website[16] as a CSV file.

Warning: Gotchas ahead!

Be careful, though, as not all CSV files are created equal. Perhaps because of the way I processed the file I got, I ran into a couple of frustrating problems within Python.

For one thing, some of the column header names somehow became "corrupted" with an extra space. That made it impossible for Pandas to successfully parse my data, returning a confusing error message:

[16]https://www.wsj.com/market-data/quotes/index/SPX/historical-prices

```
KeyError: "['Low', 'High', 'Open', 'Close'] not in \
index"
```

"Not in index"? But of course they're all in the index. What foolishness!

Well, in fact, "Low " (with a space) *was* in the index, but "Low" (without a space) was nowhere to be found. I had to open the CSV file in a plain text editor to properly remove those spaces.

My second problem was the result of the Date column in the CSV being read as regular strings. This prevented Pandas from properly sequencing the events by date. This gave the resulting graphs the disturbing (and misleading) sense that we've been inexorably heading into a major depression for the past two decades - with the S&P crashing from 3700 down to around 800!

Reformatting and then sorting the CSV by Date in my Libre-Office Calc software solved that problem.

You may not face those exact problems, but you can be sure that you'll eventually confront data sources suffering from some kind of corruption. So keep your eyes open.

At any rate, here's how I read the CSV file into a dataframe:

```
sp = pd.read_csv('new_s_p_500.csv')
```

This dataframe is so much larger than either of the other two I've worked with because it contains stock quotes for *each day* of the past 20 years. That's obviously far more than we'll need. And it'll also make calibrating the new data with my CPI and wages data series harder.

So I'm going to reformat the data in the Date column to look more like the raw data we got from our two BLS resources, and then remove all rows besides a single quarterly quote. We'll obviously lose an awful lot of the precision in this data set, but that's not what we're after here anyway.

I'll start by making sure the column uses the `datetime64` format. Then I'll use `strftime` to organize the dates so the year comes first, followed by month and day. Along the way, I'll also set the dash character `-` as the delimiter.

```
sp['Date'] = sp['Date'].astype('datetime64[ns]')
sp['Date'] = sp['Date'].dt.strftime('%Y-%m-%d')
```

Now I'll use `str.replace` in much the same way I did for the wages data to reformat all the quarterly quotes as the "year" plus, say, "Q1".

```
sp['Date'] = sp['Date'].str.replace('-03-30', 'Q1')
sp['Date'] = sp['Date'].str.replace('-06-30', 'Q2')
sp['Date'] = sp['Date'].str.replace('-09-30', 'Q3')
sp['Date'] = sp['Date'].str.replace('-12-31', 'Q4')
```

That shouldn't be new to you at this point. Nor should the next step: filtering the entire data series and keeping only those rows that contain a "Q".

```
sp = sp[(sp.Date.str.contains("Q") == True)]
```

I'll wrap up our CSV manipulation by selecting only the `Date` and `Close` columns to populate the `sp1` variable. Why `Close` and not `Open` or `High`, etc? No reason at all. As long as we're consistent, I don't believe it'll make all that much difference either way.

```
sp1 = sp[['Date', 'Close']]
sp1.head()
```

```
        Date        Close
187     2002Q3      815.28
251     2002Q4      879.82
375     2003Q2      974.50
439     2003Q3      995.97
503     2003Q4      1111.92
```

Looking through the data will show you that some quarters are actually missing. I'll let you figure out why that is (hint: you'll need some very basic general domain knowledge to figure it out).

Now that we've got our S&P quotes all nice and comfy in a dataframe, what should we do with them? My first impulse was to throw all three of our data sets into a single plot so we can compare them. That was a terrible idea, but let's see it through anyway so we can learn why.

The way we merged our first two data sets into a single dataframe earlier won't work here. But getting it done the right way isn't at all difficult. I'll have to import a new tool called `reduce` that'll help. First, thought, I'll create a new dataframe made up of each of our three existing sets.

```
from functools import reduce
dfs = [newcpi, newwages, sp1]
```

Now I can use `reduce` to merge the three sets within `dfs` with the common `Date` column acting as a single index.

```
df_triple = reduce(lambda left,right:
                     pd.merge(left,right,on='Date'), \
dfs)
```

And with that, we're all set to plot our triple-set monster:

```
ax = df_triple.plot(kind='line', figsize=(20, 7))
ax.set_ylabel('S&P, CPI, and Wages')
ax.set_xlabel('Dates')
ax.grid()
```

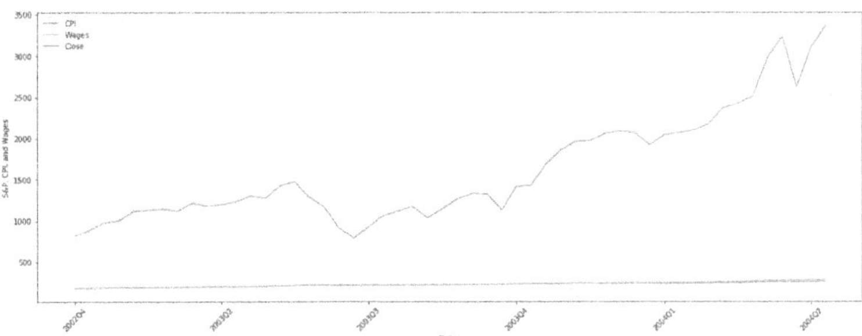

Ouch. The first - and smaller - problem is that the x-axis labels are out of sync with the actual data. That's because line plots are normally used to represent sequential, numeric data that won't require step-by-step labelling. Our 2002Q4 labels just weren't what Python was expecting.

But the bigger issue is that, as a way to visually compare our data sets, this is pretty much unusable. That's because the S&P data is on a hugely different scale (ranging between 800 and 3400), making differences between the CPI and wages sets nearly invisible.

I suppose we could play with the scale of the S&P data, perhaps dividing all the numbers by, say, 10. But why bother?

We can simply generate two graphs, one beneath the other. Even better: let's stick to bars for the S&P graph. Here's the code for an S&P visualization, followed by the graph itself:

```
ax = sp1.plot(kind='bar', figsize=(20, 7))
ax.set_xticklabels(sp1.Date, rotation=45)
ax.set_ylabel('S&P Index quotes by month')
ax.set_xlabel('Dates')
```

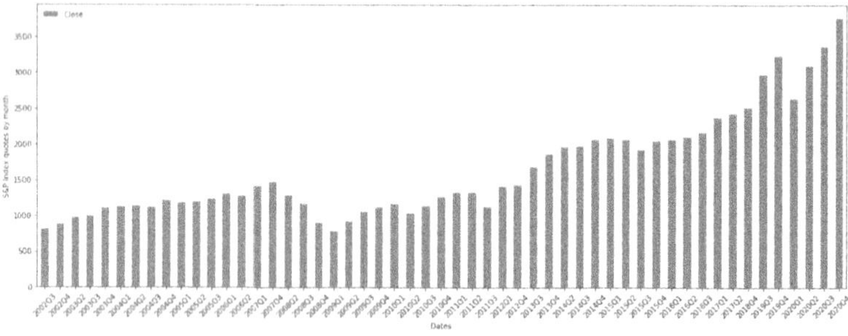

And here's how the CPI/wages graph will go:

```
ax = merged_data.plot(kind='line', figsize=(20, 7))
ax.set_xticklabels(merged_data.Date, rotation=45)
ax.set_ylabel('CPI vs. Wages and salaries - 12-mont\
h change')
ax.set_xlabel('Dates')
```

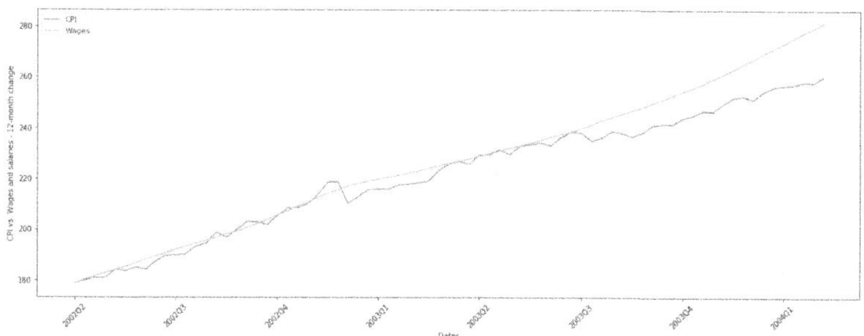

Calculate rate of increase for both CPI and S&P

I'll let you look at those two graphs and identify the key overlaps - and the events that caused them. But there is one more insight I'd like to pull from all that data: how do the Compound Annual Growth Rates (CAGR) compare between our three data sets?

The CAGR is a useful number that can, at a glance, show us how long-term investments generated (or lost) value incrementally over many years.

Of course, technically, compounded growth rates don't really make sense in the context of the CPI or even wages. After all, neither measures value that's reinvested into a sustained pool. But it will allow us to make an apples-to-apples comparison to a market investment.

I'm going to take the simple route and, one at a time, manually insert the first and last values of our three data sets. The period (in years) we're working with is 20.

```
first = 815.28
last = 3756.07
periods = 20

def CAGR(first, last, periods):
    return (last/first)**(1/periods)-1

print ('The S&P had a CAGR of {:.2%} '.format(CAGR(\
first, last, periods)))

The S&P had a CAGR of 7.94%

first = 178.8
last = 260.28
periods = 20

def CAGR(first, last, periods):
    return (last/first)**(1/periods)-1

print ('The Consumer Price Index had a CAGR of {:.2\
%}
       '.format(CAGR(first, last, periods)))

The Consumer Price Index had a CAGR of 1.90%

first = 178.64
last = 281.31
periods = 20

def CAGR(first, last, periods):
    return (last/first)**(1/periods)-1

print ('Wages had a CAGR of {:.2%} '.format(CAGR(fi\
```

```
rst, last, periods)))
```

```
Wages had a CAGR of 2.30%
```

So our (artificially inflated) consumer price index growth rate over the past 20 years was 1.9% and the (similarly artificially inflated) employment wages rate was 2.3%. While, over the same time, the S&P 500 market index increased at an average *annual* rate of 7.94%!

Am I suggesting that owning Exchange Traded Funds (ETFs) built to mirror the S&P 500 assets basket over the long term is a good investment strategy? Well, you should be aware that I'm entirely unqualified as a financial advisor and, in any case, this chapter is focused on data analytics, not investment guidance.

But in answer to the question: Yes.

Working With Major US Storm Data

Sometimes it can be somehow comforting to reflect on how much worse everything is now than in the good old days. Kids have no respect, everything costs way too much, public officials don't inspire trust, and even the weather: we never *used* to get so many devastating hurricanes, did we?

Well I'm old enough to have been around the block a few times and I'm not sure. I wasn't exactly angelic as a child, things *always* cost more than we wanted them to, and public officials were never the most loved creatures on the planet. But major storms? I haven't a clue.

It turns out that there's a lot of excellent storm data out there, so there's no reason why we shouldn't at least search for some clues. First, though, we should carefully define some terms and fill in some background details.

What Is a Major Storm?

Hurricanes - or, more accurately, tropical cyclones - are "tropical" in the sense that they form over oceans within tropical regions. The term "tropics" refers to the area of the earth's surface that falls within 23 degrees (or so) of the equator, to both its north and south. The storms are called "cyclones" because the movement of their winds is cyclical (clockwise in the Southern Hemisphere and counterclockwise in the Northern Hemisphere).

Cyclones are fed by evaporated ocean water and leave torrential and often violent thunderstorms in their wake - especially after drifting over habited land areas.

In broad terms, a storm producing sustained winds of between around 34 and 63 knots (or between 39 and 72 miles per hour) is considered a tropical storm. Storms with winds above 64 knots (73 mph) are hurricanes (or, in the Western Pacific or North Indian Oceans, typhoons).

Hurricanes are measured by categories between one and five, where category five hurricanes are the most violent and dangerous.

Where Does Major Storm Data Come From?

Reliable and largely consistent historical storm data exists, at least in the US, for the past century and a half. But properly understanding the context of that data will require some knowledge of how those observations were made over the years.

Until the 1940's, most observations were made by the crews of ocean-going ships. But ship's crews can only observe and report what they see, and what they see will be determined by where they go. Before the opening of the Panama Canal in 1914, ships travelling between Europe and the Pacific ocean would follow a route around the southern tip of South America that largely missed US coastal areas. As a result, it's likely that a significant percentage of weather events were simply missed.

Similarly, the advent of aircraft reconnaissance in the 1940s would have allowed scientists to catch more events that would have earlier been missed. And the use of weather satellites from the 1960s on has allowed us to catch just about all ocean activity.

These changes, and their impact on storm data, are neatly summarized on this page[17] from the US government National Oceanic and Atmospheric Administration (NOAA) site, based on a data analysis study[18] performed for the Geophysical Fluid Dynamics Laboratory (GFDL).

What Does the Historical Record Show?

So after all that background, what does the data actually say? Are serious hurricanes more common now than in the past? Well, according to the NOAA website, the answer is: "No." Here's how they put it[19]:

> "Atlantic tropical storms lasting more than 2 days have not increased in number. Storms lasting less than two days have increased sharply, but this is likely due to better observations...We are unaware of a climate change signal that would result in an

[17]https://www.gfdl.noaa.gov/historical-atlantic-hurricane-and-tropical-storm-records/

[18]https://www.gfdl.noaa.gov/wp-content/uploads/files/user_files/gav/publications/vk_08_recount.pdf

[19]https://www.gfdl.noaa.gov/historical-atlantic-hurricane-and-tropical-storm-records/

> increase of only the shortest duration storms, while such an increase is qualitatively consistent with what one would expect from improvements with observational practices."

You'll get the whole story, including a nice explanation for the data manipulation choices they made, by reading the study itself. In fact, I encourage you to read that study, because it's a great example of how the professionals approach data problems.

From here on in, however, you'll be stuck with my amateur and simplified attempts to visualize the raw, unadjusted data record.

US Hurricane Data: 1851-2019

Our source for "Continental United States Hurricane Impacts/Landfalls" data is this NOAA webpage[20]. To download the data, I simply copied it by clicking my mouse at the top left (the "Year" heading field) and dragging all the way down to the bottom-right. I then pasted it into a plain-text editor on my local computer and saved it to a file with the extension `.csv`.

Cleaning Up the Hurricane Data

If you quickly look through the webpage itself you'll see some formatting that'll need cleaning up. Each decade is introduced with a single row containing nothing but a string looking like: `1850s`. We'll want to just drop those rows. Years with no

---

[20]https://www.aoml.noaa.gov/hrd/hurdat/All_U.S._Hurricanes.html

events contain the string `none` in the second column. Those, too, will need to go.

There are some events that apparently have no data for their Max Wind speeds. Instead of a number (measured in knots), the speed values for those events are represented by five dashes (`-----`). We'll have to convert that to something we can work with.

And finally, while months are generally represented by three-letter abbreviations, there were a couple of events that stretched across two months. So we'll be able to properly process those, I'll therefore convert `Sp-Oc` and `Jl-Au` to `Sep` and `Jul` respectively. The fact is that we won't actually be using the month column, so this won't really make any difference. But it's a good tool to know.

Here's how we set things up in Jupyter:

```
import pandas as pd
import matplotlib as plt
import matplotlib.pyplot as plt
import numpy as np

df = pd.read_csv('all-us-hurricanes-noaa.csv')
```

Let's look at the data types for each column. We can ignore the strings in the States and Name column - we're not interested in those anyway. But we will need to do something with the date and Max Wind columns - they won't do us any good as `object`.

```
df.dtypes
```

```
Year                                                object
Month                                               object
States Affected and Category by States              object
Highest\nSaffir-\nSimpson\nU.S. Category           float64
Central Pressure\n(mb)                             float64
Max Wind\n(kt)                                      object
Name                                                object
dtype: object
```

So I'll filter all rows in the `Year` column for the letter `s` and simply drop them (`== False`). That will take care of all the decade headers (i.e., those rows containing an `s` as part of something like `1850s`).

I'll similarly drop rows containing the string `None` in the `Month` column to eliminate years without storm events. While quiet years could have some impact on our visualizations, I suspect that including them with some kind of null value would probably skew things even more the other way. They'd also greatly complicate our visualizations. Finally, I'll replace those two multi-month rows.

```
df = df[(df.Year.str.contains("s")) == False]
df = df[(df.Month.str.contains("None")) == False]
df = df.replace('Sp-Oc','Sep')
df = df.replace('Jl-Au','Jul')
```

Next, I'll use the handy Pandas `to-datetime` method to convert the three-letter month abbreviations to numbers between 1 and 12. The format code `%b` is one of Python's legal date-related designations and tells Python that we're working with a three-letter abbreviation. For the full list, see this page.[21]

```
df.Month = pd.to_datetime(df.Month, format='%b').dt\
.month
```

I'd like to tighten up the headers a bit so they're a bit easier to both read and reference in our code. `df.columns` will change all column header values to the list I specify here:

```
df.columns =['Year', 'Month', 'States', 'Category',
             'Pressure', 'Max Wind', 'Name']
```

I'll have to convert the Year data from string objects to integers, or Python won't know how to work with them appropriately. That's done using `astype`. As advertised, I'll also convert the null (`-----`) values in `Max Wind` to `NaN` - which NumPy will read as "not a number." I'll then convert the data in `Max Wind` from `object` to `float`.

```
df = df.astype({'Year': 'int'})
df = df.replace('-----',np.NaN)
df = df.astype({'Max Wind': 'float'})
```

Let's see how all that looks now:

[21]https://www.w3schools.com/python/gloss_python_date_format_codes.asp

```
df.dtypes
```

```
Year           int64
Month          int64
States        object
Category     float64
Pressure     float64
Max Wind     float64
Name          object
dtype: object
```

Much better.

Presenting Hurricane Data

Now, looking at our data, I'm going to suggest that we break out the three metrics: hurricane category, barometric pressure, and maximum wind speeds. My thinking is that there's little to gain from the added complication by lumping them together, and we risk losing sight of important differences between incidents of lighter and more serious storms.

Of course, I can always isolate individual metrics to see what their distributions would look like. Using `value_counts` against the `Category` column, for instance, shows me that the lighter category 1 and 2 hurricanes are far more frequent than the more dangerous events.

```
df['Category'].value_counts()
```

```
1.0    121
2.0     83
3.0     62
4.0     25
5.0      4
Name: Category, dtype: int64
```

And plotting a single histogram of the complete data set does give us a nice overview of the number of events (represented on the y-axis) through history, but we might be losing some of the finer details in the process.

From this histogram, it's obvious that there's been no noticeable change in storm frequency over time. To be sure that my choice of the number of bins we're using isn't unintentionally masking important trends, experiment with other values besides 25.

```
df.hist(column='Year', bins=25)
```

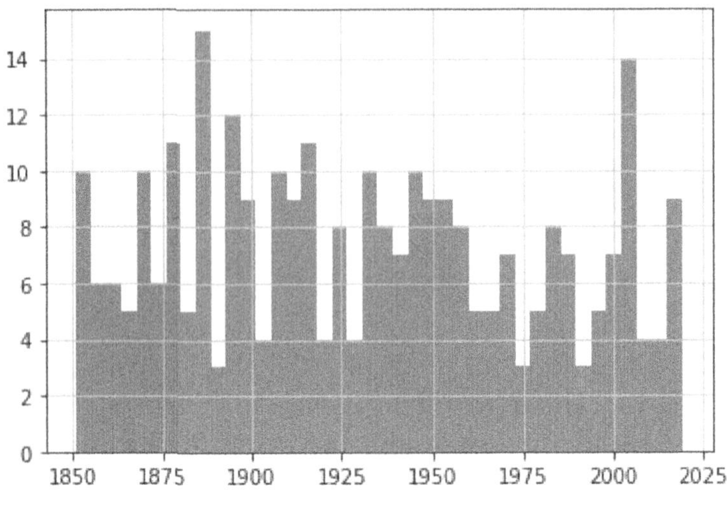

All Hurricane Events

But to allow us to focus on each metric, I'll plot three separate graphs. To do that, I'll create three new dataframes and populate each one with the contents of the `Year` column and the respective data column.

```
df_category = df[['Year','Category']]
df_wind = df[['Year','Max Wind']]
df_pressure = df[['Year','Pressure']]
```

Sending each of those dataframes straight to a plot will miss the point, because it won't distinguish between the severity of storms. So I'll show you how we can break out the data by category (1-5). This `for` loop will iterate through the numbers 1-6 (which is "Python" for returning the numbers between 1 and 5) and uses each of those numbers in turn to search for hurricanes of that category.

Rows whose category matches the number will be written to a new (temporary) dataframe called `df1` which will, in turn, be used to plot a histogram. The `plt.title` line applies a title for the printed graph that will include the category number (the current value of `converted_num`).

The loop will work through the process five times, each time writing the number of events the current category to `df1`. All five histograms will be printed, one after the other.

```
for x in range(1, 6):
    cat_num = x
    converted_num = str(cat_num)
    dfcat = df_category['Category']==(x)
    df1 = df_category[dfcat]
    df1.hist(column='Year', bins=20)
    plt.title("Total Category " + (converted_num) +\
 " Events")
```

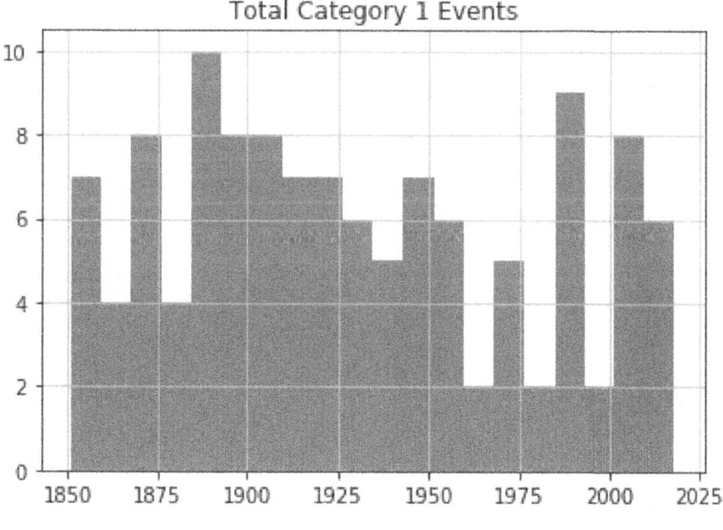

Category 1 Hurricanes

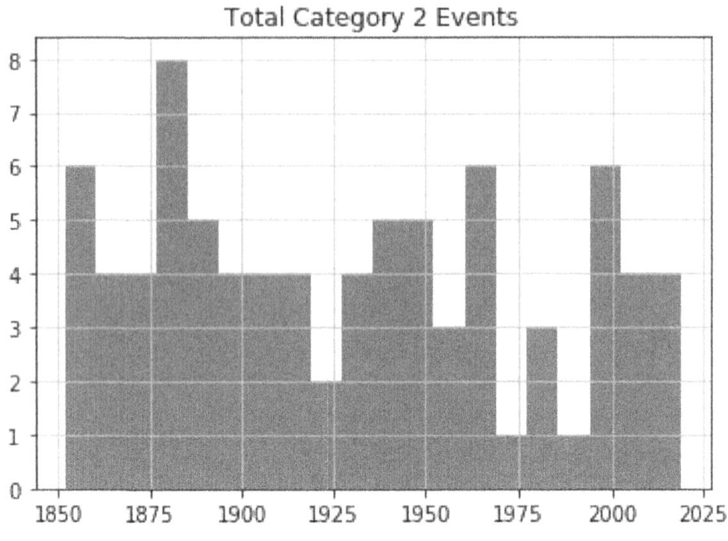

Category 2 Hurricanes

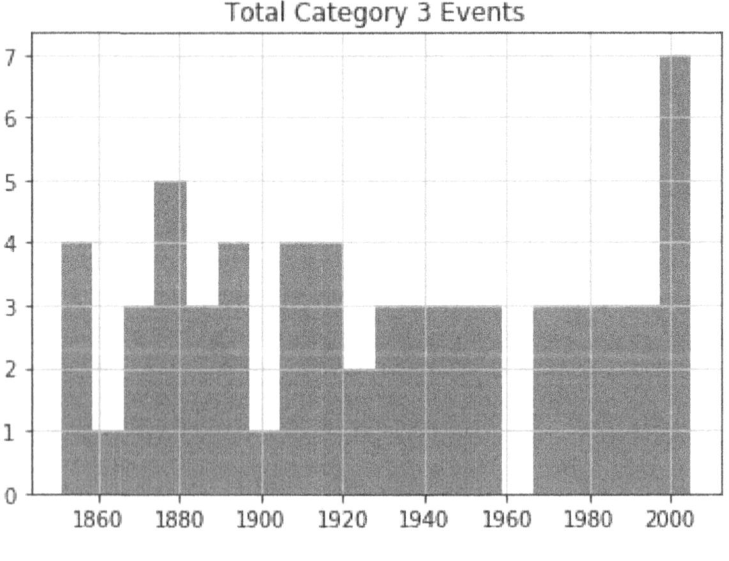

Category 3 Hurricanes

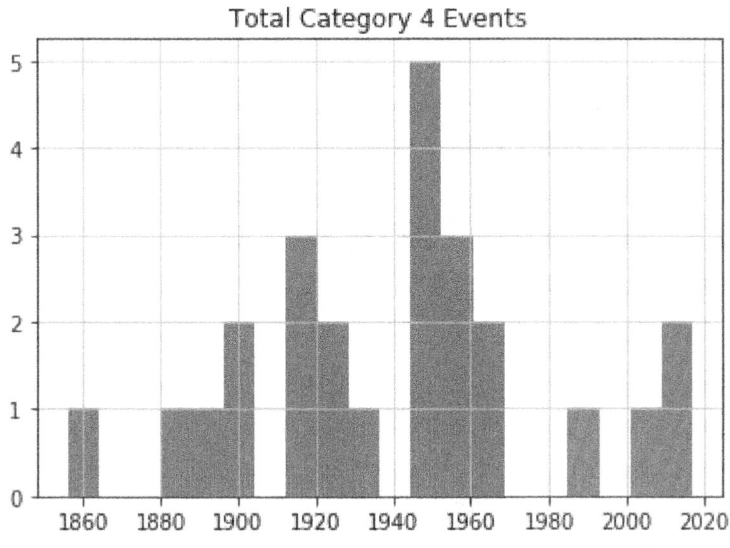

Category 4 Hurricanes

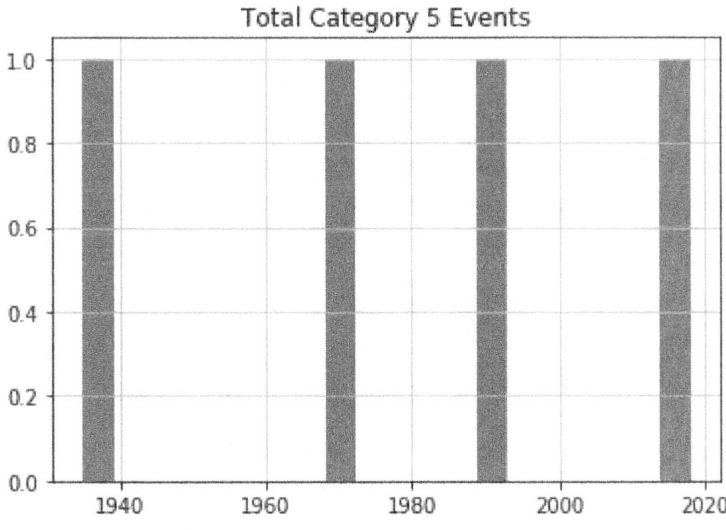

Category 5 Hurricanes

As you can see, there's no noticeable evidence of significantly rising storm frequency over time.

As always, scan your data (using tools like `value_counts()`) to confirm that the plots make sense in the real world.

US Tropical Storm Data: 1851-1965, 1983-2019

Hurricanes (or cyclones) are, of course, only one part of the story. A rise in the frequency of destructive tropical storms would also be cause for concern. Fortunately, NOAA makes relevant data available in much the same format as their hurricane data. Here's the webpage[22] where you'll find the chart. Copy the data into a `.csv` file the same way as before.

Note, however, how there's no data for the years 1966-1982. Don't ask me why. There just isn't. Funny thing, weather.

I would create a new Jupyter notebook for this part of the project. There's nothing we'll need from the hurricane version. Therefore, you'll set things up as always:

```
import pandas as pd
import matplotlib as plt
import numpy as np
df = pd.read_csv('all-us-tropical-storms-noaa.csv')
```

Cleaning Up the Hurricane Data

The rows representing years without events should, again, be removed:

[22] https://www.aoml.noaa.gov/hrd/hurdat/uststorms.html

```
df = df[(df.Date.str.contains("None")) == False]
```

The `Date` column in this dataset has characters pointing to five footnotes: $, *, #, %, and &. The footnotes contain important information, but those characters will give us grief if we don't remove them. These commands will get that done, replacing all such strings in the `Date` column with nothing:

```
df['Date'] = df.Date.str.replace('\$', '')
df['Date'] = df.Date.str.replace('\*', '')
df['Date'] = df.Date.str.replace('\#', '')
df['Date'] = df.Date.str.replace('\%', '')
df['Date'] = df.Date.str.replace('\&', '')
```

Next, I'll reset the column headers. First, because it will be easier to work with nice, short names. But primarily because, as a Linux sysadmin, I find spaces in filenames or headings morally offensive.

```
df.columns =['Storm#', 'Date', 'Time', 'Lat', 'Lon'\
,
             'MaxWinds', 'LandfallState', 'StormNam\
e']
```

The column data types are going to need some work:

```
df.dtypes
```

```
Storm#            object
Date              object
Time              object
Lat               object
Lon               object
MaxWinds         float64
LandfallState     object
StormName         object
dtype: object
```

I'm actually not sure what those Storm # values are all about, but they're not hurting anyone. The dates are formatted much better than they were for the hurricane data. But I will need to convert them to a new format. Let's do it right and go with `datetime`.

```
df.Date = pd.to_datetime(df.Date)
```

Presenting Tropical Storm Data

For our purposes, the only data column that really matters is MaxWinds - as that, obviously, is what defines the intensity of the storm. This command will create a new dataframe made up of the `Date` and `MaxWinds` columns:

```
df1 = df[['Date','MaxWinds']]
```

No reason to push this off: we might as well fire up a histogram right away. You'll immediately see the gap around 1970 where there was no data. You'll also see that, again, there doesn't seem to be any upward trend.

```
df1['Date'].hist()
```

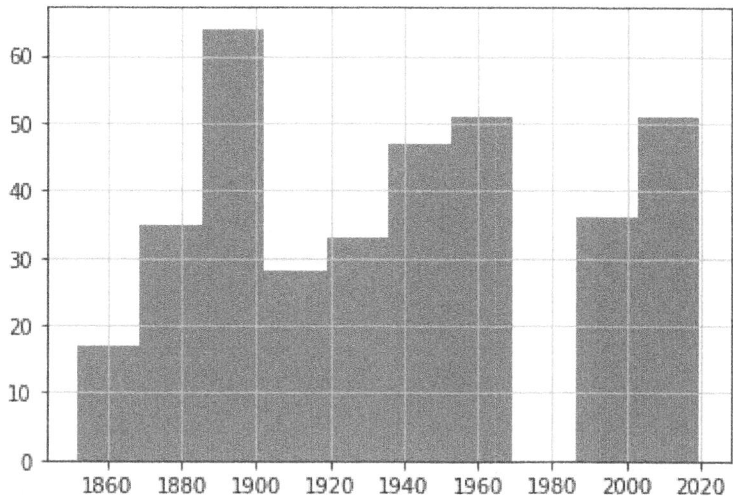

Histogram of All Tropical Storms

But we really should drill down a bit deeper here. After all, this data just mixes together 30 knot with 75 knot storms. We'll definitely want to know whether or not they're happening at similar rates.

Let's find out how many rows of data we've got. `shape` tells us that we've got 362 events altogether.

```
print(df1.shape)
```

```
(362, 2)
```

Printing our dataframe shows us that the `MaxWinds` values are all multiples of 5. If you scan the data for yourself, you'll see that they range between 30 and 70 or so.

```
df1
```

```
          Date                    MaxWinds
1          1851-10-19          50.0
6          1856-08-19          50.0
7          1857-09-30          50.0
8          1858-09-14          60.0
9          1858-09-16          50.0
...          ...          ...
391          2017-09-27          45.0
392          2018-05-28          40.0
393          2018-09-03          45.0
394          2018-09-03          45.0
395          2019-09-17          40.0
362 rows Ã— 2 columns
```

So let's divide our data into four smaller sets as reasonable proxies for storms of various levels of intensity. I've created four dataframes and populated them with events falling in their narrower ranges (i.e., between 30 and 39 knots, 40 and 49, 50 and 59, and 60 and 79). This should give us a reasonable frame of reference for our events.

```
df_30 = df1[df1['MaxWinds'].between(30, 39)]
df_40 = df1[df1['MaxWinds'].between(40, 49)]
df_50 = df1[df1['MaxWinds'].between(50, 59)]
df_60 = df1[df1['MaxWinds'].between(60, 79)]
```

Let's confirm that the cut-off points we've chosen make sense. This code will attractively print the number of rows in the index of each of our four dataforms.

```
st1 = len(df_30.index)
print('The number of storms between 30 and 39: ', s\
t1)
st2 = len(df_40.index)
print('The number of storms between 40 and 49: ', s\
t2)
st3 = len(df_50.index)
print('The number of storms between 50 and 59: ', s\
t3)
st4 = len(df_60.index)
print('The number of storms between 60 and 79: ', s\
t4)
```

```
The number of storms between 30 and 39:  51
The number of storms between 40 and 49:  113
The number of storms between 50 and 59:  142
The number of storms between 60 and 79:  56
```

There's probably an elegant way to combine those four commands into one. But my philosophy is that syntax that would take me an hour to figure out will never outweigh the simplicity of five seconds of cutting and pasting. Ever.

We could also look just a bit deeper into the data using our old friend, `value_counts()`. This will show us that there were 71 40 knot events and 42 45 knot events throughout our time range.

```
df_40['MaxWinds'].value_counts()
```

```
40.0    71
45.0    42
Name: MaxWinds, dtype: int64
```

We can plot a single line graph to display all four of our subsets together. This plot adds axis and plot labels and a legend to make the data easier to understand. The `subplot(111)` value controls the size of the figure.

```
import matplotlib.pyplot as plt
fig = plt.figure()
ax = plt.subplot(111)
df_30['MaxWinds'].plot(ax=ax, label='df_30')
df_40['MaxWinds'].plot(ax=ax, label='df_40')
df_50['MaxWinds'].plot(ax=ax, label='df_50')
df_60['MaxWinds'].plot(ax=ax, label='df_60')
ax.set_ylabel('Wind Speed In Knots')
ax.set_xlabel('Time Between 1851 and 2019')
plt.title('Tropical Storms by Maximum Wind Speeds (\
knots)')
ax.legend()
```

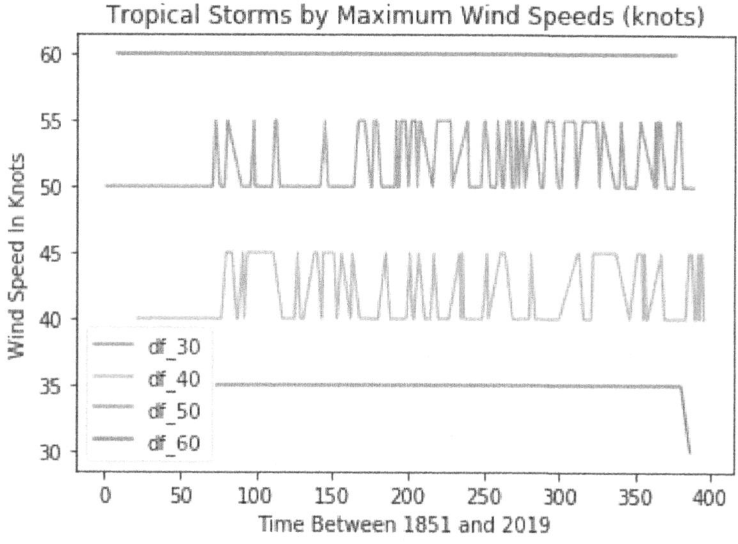

All Tropical Storms

This can be helpful for confirming that we're not making a mess of the data itself. Checking visually will show, for instance, that there was, indeed, only a single 30 knot event in our dataset and that it took place towards the end of our time frame in 2016. But it's not a great way to show us changes in event frequency.

For that, we'll look at the data held in each of our dataframes.

```
df_30['Date'].hist(bins=20)
```

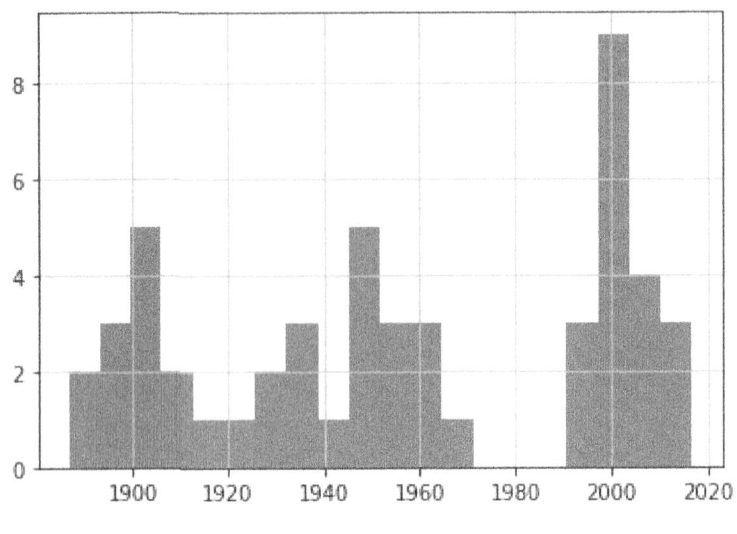

30-39 Knot Events

```
df_40['Date'].hist(bins=20)
```

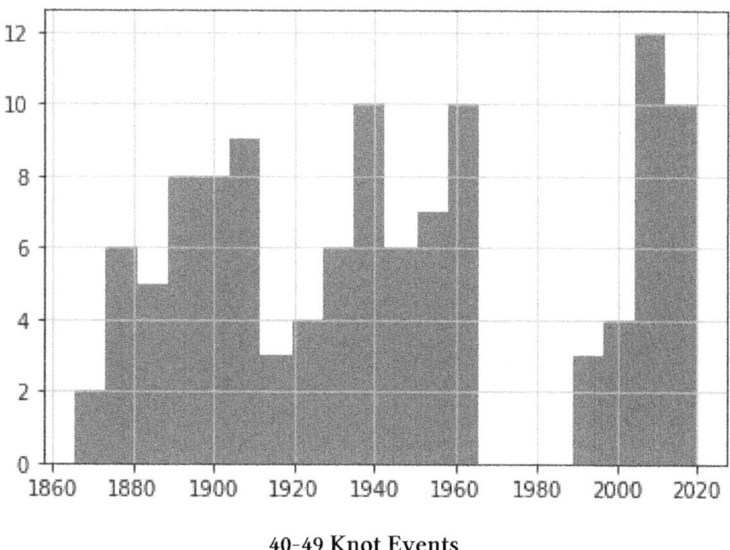

40-49 Knot Events

```
df_50['Date'].hist(bins=20)
```

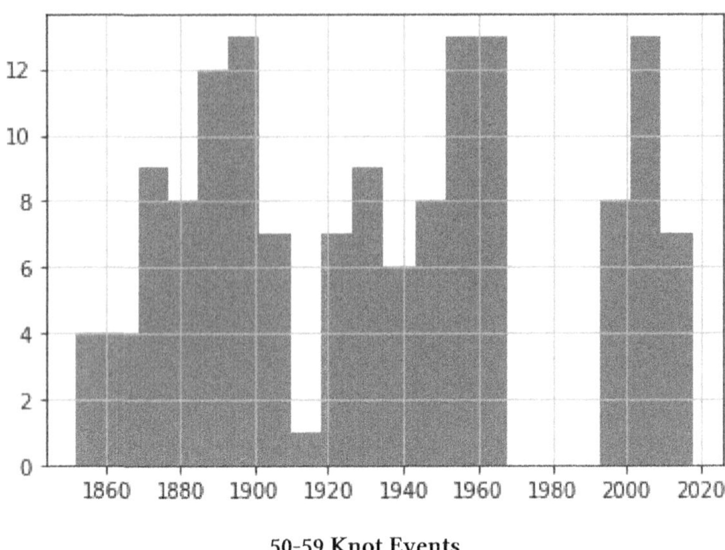

50-59 Knot Events

```
df_60['Date'].hist(bins=20)
```

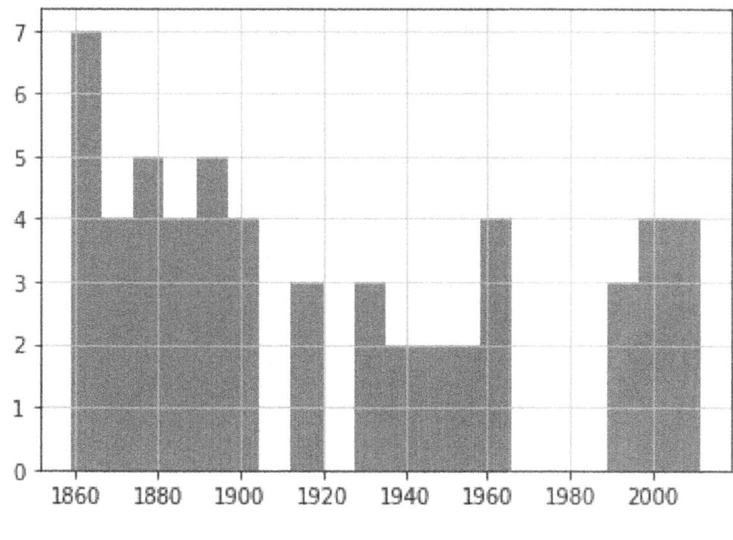

60-79 Knot Events

A quick glance through those four plots shows us fairly consistent event frequency through the 150 years or so of our data. Again, try it yourself using different numbers of bins to make sure we're not missing some important trends.

Property Rights and Economic Development

What defines a successful society? I'm sure you've got a pretty good idea what you'd like to be and what you think is the best way to get there. But finding some objective way to measure the success of large populations is much harder.

Economists - being incurable card-carrying data geeks - like to use statistics and financial models as proxies for social success. So let's see if we can use some of those numbers to inspire useful insights into the problem. In particular, we're going to look for possible correlations between specific social conditions on one side, and successful economic outcomes on the other.

How Do You Measure Conditions and Outcomes?

Let's look at outcomes first. One very popular way to assess the economic health of a country is through its gross domestic product (GDP). The GDP is the total value of everything produced within a country's borders. In theory at least, this number is important. That's because the higher the GDP - meaning, the more production that's happening - the more access to capital, employment opportunities, and variety of available consumption choices your citizens will enjoy.

Of course, that's completely true only in theory. In the real world, the benefits of a strong GDP won't have an equal impact on every individual. There will always be people who won't find suitable work in a given economy. And not everyone defines their success through the consumption of material goods.

Still, GDP is a reasonable place to at least begin our analysis.

Now what about measuring the *underlying economic conditions* that are responsible for economic health? This one can be tricky. Just what *are* the conditions that lie behind the widest possible enjoyment economic success?

I'm not aware of any *single* metric that'll provide this insight. But there have been attempts to build a set of metrics to approximate the kind of rights and freedoms that common sense suggests should accompany a healthy society.

One such attempt is the annual Index of Economic Freedom[23]. The index's overall score is made up of assessments of a basket of freedoms, including labor, business, spending, and trade, along with other measures like government integrity and respect for property rights.

What makes just those rights and freedoms important? Well, focusing specifically on property rights, imagine how difficult life would be if:

- You had no way of reliably proving that the home you purchased was really yours

[23]https://www.heritage.org/index/explore?u=637470799817780528

- You had no way of reliably proving that the merchandise you purchased for your grocery store was really yours
- You had no way of reliably proving that the royalty rights to the book you wrote are yours
- You had no confidence that the money in your bank account won't be seized at any moment

Without reliable and enforceable proof, any government or bank official - or any individual off the street - could seize your property at any time. Of course, we can all choose to share our property with the community - as many do through the Creative Commons license[24] - but it should be through choice, not force.

Whatever you think about materialism, living in a society where property rights aren't respected breeds insecurity. And that's not a recipe for any kind of success.

Getting the Data

You can get up-to-date GDP data by country from many sources. This Wikipedia page[25], for instance, includes per capita GDP numbers from three different sources: The International Monetary Fund (IMF), the World Bank, and the CIA World Factbook.

We'll want our data broken down to the per capita level because that's the best way to get useful apples-to-apples comparisons between countries of different sizes.

[24] https://creativecommons.org/
[25] https://en.wikipedia.org/wiki/List_of_countries_by_GDP_(PPP)

I got my GDP data from the World Bank site, on this page[26]. My Index of Economic Freedom data I took from here[27].

Here's how all the basic setup works in a Jupyter notebook:

```
import pandas as pd
import numpy as np
import matplotlib as plt
import matplotlib.pyplot as plt

gdp = pd.read_csv('WorldBank_per_capita_GDP.csv')
ec_index = pd.read_csv('heritage-all-data.csv')
```

Running gdp shows us that the GDP data set has got 248 rows that include plenty of stuff we don't want; like some null values (NaN) and at least a few rows at the end with general values that will get in the way of our focus on countries. We'll need to clean all that up, but our code will simply ignore those general values, because there will be no corresponding rows in the ec_index dataframe.

```
gdp
```

```
        Country Year Value
0        Afghanistan        2019.0 2156.4
1        Albania        2019.0 14496.1
2        Algeria        2019.0 12019.9
3        American Samoa NaN NaN
4        Andorra NaN NaN
...        ...        ...        ...
243        Low & middle income 2019.0 11102.4
```

[26]https://data.worldbank.org/indicator/NY.GDP.PCAP.PP.CD
[27]https://www.heritage.org/index/explore?u=637470799817780528

```
244         Low income        2019.0 2506.9
245         Lower middle income 2019.0 6829.8
246         Middle income 2019.0 12113.2
247         Upper middle income 2019.0 17487.0
248 rows x 3 columns
```

`dtypes` shows us that the Year and Value columns are already formatted as float64, which is perfect for us.

```
gdp.dtypes
```

```
Country      object
Year        float64
Value       float64
dtype: object
```

We should also check the column data types used in our Index of Economic Freedom dataframe. The only three columns we'll be interested in here are `Name` (which holds country names) and `Index Year` (because there are multiple years of data included), and `Overall Score`.

```
ec_index.dtypes
```

```
Name                           object
Index Year                      int64
Overall Score                 float64
Property Rights               float64
Judicial Effectiveness        float64
Government Integrity          float64
Tax Burden                    float64
Government Spending           float64
```

```
Fiscal Health              float64
Business Freedom           float64
Labor Freedom              float64
Monetary Freedom           float64
Trade Freedom              float64
Investment Freedom         float64
Financial Freedom          float64
dtype: object
```

I'll select just the columns from both dataframes that we'll need:

```
ec_index = ec_index[['Name', 'Index Year', 'Overall\
 Score']]
gdp = gdp[['Country', 'Value']]
```

I'll then rename the columns in the ec_index dataframe. The critical one is changing `Name` to `Country` so it matches the column name in the gdp dataframe. If we don't do that, it'll be much harder to align the two data sets.

```
ec_index.columns = ['Country', 'Year', 'Score']
```

Next, I'll limit the data we take from ec_index to only those rows whose Year column covers 2019.

```
ec_index = ec_index[ec_index.Year.isin(["2019"])]
```

Now I'll merge the two dataframes, telling Pandas to use the values of Country to align the data. When that's done, I'll select only those columns that we still need: to exclude the Year column from ec_index and then remove rows with NaN values. That'll be all the data cleaning we'll need here.

```
merged_data = pd.merge(gdp, ec_index, on='Country')
merged_data = merged_data[['Country', 'Value', 'Sco\
re']]
merged_data.dropna(axis=0, how='any', thresh=None,
                   subset=None, inplace=True)
```

Visualizing Data Sets Using Scatter Plots

It's not uncommon for data cleaning to take up more time and effort than the actual visualization. This will be a perfect example. Just this simple, single line of code will give us a lot of what we're after:

```
plt.scatter(merged_data.Score, merged_data.Value)
```

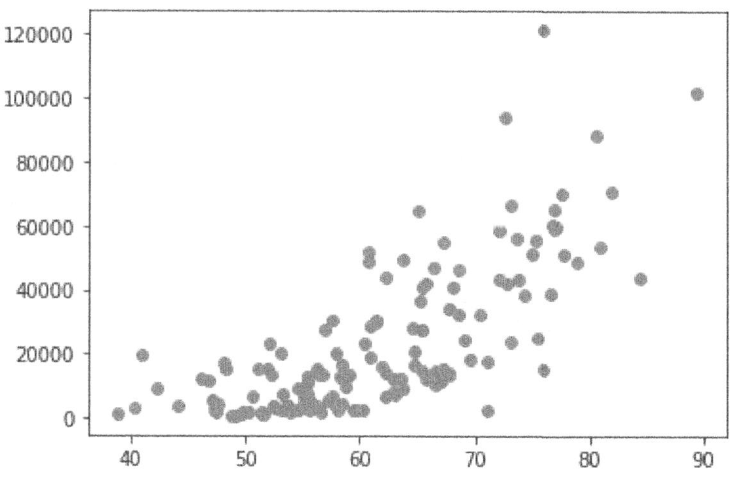

A simple scatter plot showing countries' index scores on the x-axis and GDP on the y-axis

What that did was take the two data points (GDP and index) for each country and plot a dot at its intersection point. The higher a country's index score, the further along to the right it's dot will appear. And the higher its per capita GDP, the higher up the y-axis it'll be.

If there were absolutely no correlation between a country's GDP and its index score (or, in other words, the economic freedoms had no impact on production) then you would expect to see the dots spread randomly across both axes. The fact that we can easily see a pattern - the dots are clearly trending towards the top-right of the chart - tells us that higher index scores tend to predict higher GDP.

Of course there are anomalies in our data. There are countries whose position appears way out of range of all the others. It would be nice if we could somehow see which countries those are. And it would also be nice if we could quantify the precise statistical relationship between our two values, rather than having to visually guess. I'll show you how those work in just a moment.

But first, one very small detour. Like everything else in the technology world, there are many ways to get a task done in Python. Here's a second code snippet that'll generate the exact same output:

```
x = merged_data.Score
y = merged_data.Value
plt.scatter(x,y)
```

There will be times when using that second style will make it easier to add features to your output. But the choice is yours.

Adding "Hover" Visibility

Now let me get back to visualizing those anomalies in our data - and better understanding the data as a whole. To make this happen, I'll import another couple of libraries that are part of the Plotly family of tools. You may need to manually install on your host using `pip install plotly` before these will work. Here's what we'll need to import:

```
import plotly.graph_objs as go
import plotly.express as px
```

From there, we can run `px.scatter` and point it to our `merged_data` dataframe, associating the Score column with the x-axis, and Value with the y-axis. So we'll be able to hover over a dot and see the data it represents, we'll add the `hover_data` argument and tell it to include Country and Score data.

```
fig = px.scatter(merged_data, x="Score", y="Value",\
 log_x=True,
                hover_data=["Country", "Score"])
fig.show()
```

This time, when you run the code, you get the same nice plot. But if you hover your mouse over any dot, you'll also see its data values. In this example, we can see that the tiny - but rich - country of Luxembourg has an economic freedom score of 75.9 and a per capita GDP of more than 121 thousand dollars.

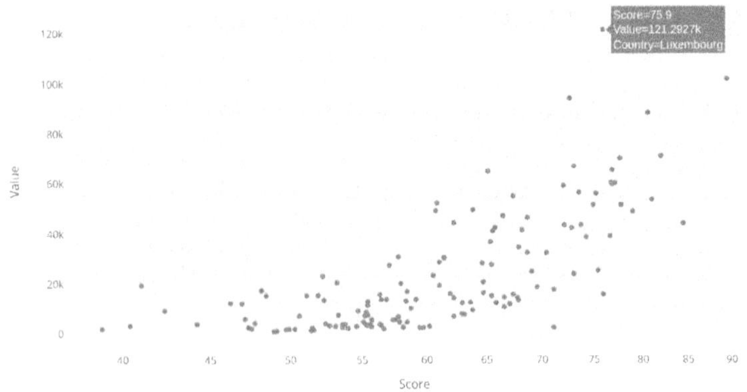

Hovering over a dot reveals associated data

That's an important functionality, particularly when it comes to quickly identifying statistical outliers like Luxembourg.

Adding a Regression Line

There's one more important piece of information that'll improve how we understand our data: its R-squared value.

We already saw how our plot showed a visible trend up and to the right. But, as we also saw, there were outliers. Can we be confident that the outliers are the exceptions and that the overall relationship between our two data sources is sound? There's only so much we can assume based on visually viewing a graph. At some point, we'll need hard numbers to describe what we're looking at.

A simple linear regression analysis uses a mathematical formula to provide us with such a number: `y = mx + b` - where `m` is the slope of the line, and `b` is the y-intercept. This will give us a coefficient of determination (also described as R-squared or R^2) that's a measure of the strength of the relationship between a dependent variable and the data model.

R-squared is a number between 0 and 100%, where 100% would indicate a perfect fit. Of course, in the real world, a 100% fit is next to impossible. You'll judge the accuracy of your model (or assumption) within the context of the data you're working with.

How can you add a regression line to a Pandas chart? There are, as always, many ways to go about it. Here's one I came across that, if you decide to try it, will work. But it takes way too much effort and code for my liking. It involves writing a Python function, and then calling it as part of a manual integration of the regression formula with your data.

Look through it and try it out if you like. I've got other things to do with my time.

```
def fit_line(x, y):

    x = x.to_numpy() # convert into numpy arrays
    y = y.to_numpy() # convert into numpy arrays

    A = np.vstack([x, np.ones(len(x))]).T
    m, c = np.linalg.lstsq(A, y, rcond=None)[0]

    return m, c

fig = px.scatter(merged_data, x="Score", y="Value",
                 log_x=True,
                 hover_data=["Country", "Score"])
# fit a linear model
m, c = fit_line(x = merged_data.Score,
                y = merged_data.Value)
```

```
# add the linear fit on top
fig.add_trace(
    go.Scatter(
        x=merged_data.Score,
        y=m*merged_data.Score + c,
        mode="lines",
        line=go.scatter.Line(color="red"),
        showlegend=False)
)

fig.show()
```

So what's my preferred approach? It's dead easy. Just add a `trendline` argument to the code we've already been using. That's it. `ols`, by the way, stands for "Ordinary Least Square" - which is a type of linear regression.

```
fig = px.scatter(merged_data, x="Score", y="Value",
                 trendline="ols", log_x=True,
                 hover_data=["Country", "Score"])
fig.show()
```

Here's how our chart looks with its regression line:

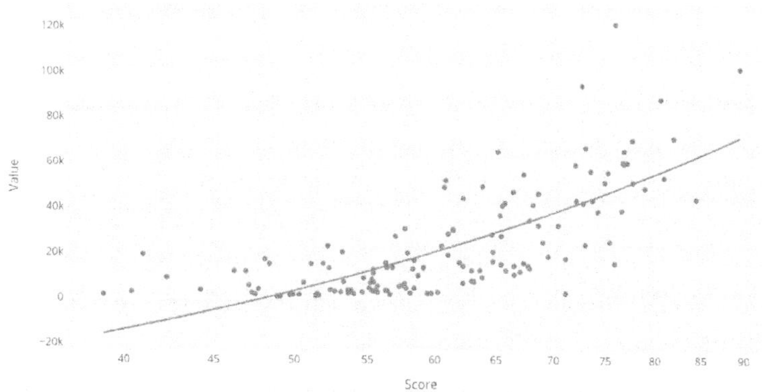

A scatter plot with a regression line

When I hover over the regression line, I'm shown an R^2 value of 0.550451. Or, in other words, around 55%. For our purposes, I'd consider that a pretty good correlation.

Other Considerations

When interpreting our plots, we should always seek to validate what we're seeing in the context of the real world. If, for instance, the data is too good to be true, then it probably isn't true.

For example, residual plots, the points that *don't* fall out right next to the regression line, should normally contain a visually random element. They should, in other words, present no visible pattern. That would suggest a bias in the data.

We should also be careful not to mix up correlation with causation. Just because, for instance, there does seem to be a demonstrable *relationship* between economic freedoms and productivity, we can't be absolutely sure which way that relationship works: do greater freedoms lead to more productivity, or does productivity (and the wealth it brings) inspire greater freedom?

In addition, as I mentioned at the start of this article, I'd like to explore other measures of social success besides GDP to see if they, too, correlate with economic freedom. One possible source of useful data might be the Organisation for Economic Co-operation and Development (OECD) and their "How's Life? Well-Being" data set[28]. But that will have to wait for another time.

[28]https://stats.oecd.org/Index.aspx?datasetcode=HSL

How Representative Is Your Government?

Is Canada's parliamentary system of government democratic?

Yes. Next question.

Ok. But how *representative* is it? Well that's something worth exploring. First, what do I mean by "representative?" It's not necessarily intuitive that all governments need to consider the will of their citizens when setting policy. I don't believe China's National People's Congress has any legal obligation to consult with its people or even consider their thoughts. Technically, our government rules in right of the sovereign of the United Kingdom and the Commonwealth realms who could, in theory, tell *us* how they'd like things run.

Through decisions made centuries ago by ancestors and predecessors of Queen Elizabeth II, our system is founded on popular elections. That means our legislators are chosen by us and, for all intents and purposes, govern in *our* right. So every few years we get to throw the old set of representatives out and choose the next one.

But what about in between elections: where do our members of parliament look for their day-to-day instructions? I believe some simple data analytics can help us answer that question. I'm going to see how often members of parliament vote strictly along party lines. If they're always following their party leaders, then it would seem it's the parties who they serve. If, on the other hand, they often cast votes independently of their parties, then they might be thinking more about their own constituents.

This won't definitively prove anything one way or the other but, if we can access a large enough data set, we should be able to draw some interesting insights.

We'll begin on a webpage managed by the House of Commons itself: Parliament's Open Data project - ourcommons.ca/en/open-data[29]. The page explains how we can make use of a freely-available application programming interface (API) to download and manipulate detailed data representing the core operations of Canada's legislature.

Like many APIs in use these days, the precise syntax you need to get the data you're after can be a bit of a puzzle. But since most programmers enjoy puzzles, this isn't a big deal. The OurCommons API expects you to play around with URLs based on the base address, `ourcommons.ca/Members/`. Adding `en` tells the server that you want service in English. Adding a forward slash and then the word `votes` means that you're looking for voting records.

Some resources are available in XML formatting, while others can be downloaded in the spreadsheet-friendly CSV format. But we're going to stick with plain old HTML for our purposes. That means any URL you see here can be loaded and enjoyed in your browser just like any other webpage.

We'll begin with the Votes page - ourcommons.ca/Members/en/votes[30]. The main data on this page consists of a table listing all the bills associated with a particular parliamentary session.

[29]https://www.ourcommons.ca/en/open-data
[30]https://www.ourcommons.ca/Members/en/votes

A *parliament*, in this context, is all the sittings occurring between the formation of a new government after one election, until its dissolution before the next election. A *session* is a few months' (or even years') worth of sittings. The second session of the 41st Parliament (which stretched from October 16 2013 until August 2, 2015) would be represented by this URL:

```
https://www.ourcommons.ca/Members/en/votes?parlSess\
ion=41-2
```

That URL would present you with links to all the votes from that session. If you preferred to see only private members' bills from that session, you could add the bill document argument: `TypeId=4`. Substituting `TypeId=3` for that, as with the next example, would return all house government bills. This example points to house government bills from the current session (the second session of the 43rd parliament):

```
https://www.ourcommons.ca/Members/en/votes?parlSess\
ion=43-2&billDocumentTypeId=3
```

If you'd prefer, you can move between views on the website itself through the various drop-down menus. But to get the sheer volume of data we're after, we'll need the power of some well-written Python code.

What's the difference between members and government bills? The former are sponsored by regular members of parliament of any party, while the latter are always sponsored by cabinet ministers and reflect the government's official position.

I would expect that parties are more likely to at least try to force the compliance of all their members when it comes to voting on government bills. Private members' bills would, perhaps, be more likely to encounter independent support or opposition. It also seems likely that we'll find more fractured voting among *opposition* parties for government bills than for members of the government. Dissension should, by that same token, be equally present within *all* parties for private members' bills.

Let's see if the data bears out our assumptions.

Scraping data from a single vote

With those introductions out of the way, let's start pulling some data. Converting the webpage for a single vote into a Pandas dataframe is surprisingly simple. After importing the Python Pandas library, I only need to pass a URL (for the seventeenth vote of the second session of the 43rd parliament, in this case) to the `pd.read_html` command. Pandas will read the page's HTML, identify data relationships, and convert everything to a table.

```
import pandas as pd
dfs = pd.read_html('https://www.ourcommons.ca/Membe\
rs/en/votes/43/2/17',header=0)
```

For some reason, the specific data we're after exists in the dataframe identified as `dfs[0]` (rather than just `dfs`). I can't say I understand why that is, but it is. So for convenience, I'll push that to the new dataframe, `df`:

```
df = dfs[0]
```

Let's see what our data looks like:

```
df.shape
(319, 4)
```

There are four columns, comprising 319 rows. That means 319 members cast votes for this bill.

To keep things clean, I'll change the names of the column headers:

```
df.columns = ['Member','Party','Vote','Paired']
```

All the votes of these first five members went against the bill ("Nay"). An affirmative vote would be identified as "Yea."

We can easily see how the party numbers broke down using the `.value_counts()` method:

```
df['Party'].value_counts().to_frame()
                Party
Liberal        146
Conservative        115
Bloc QuÃ©bÃ©cois        31
NDP                 22
Green Party         3
Independent         2
```

I'm sure you're impatiently waiting to hear how the vote went. Once again, it's `.value_counts()` to the rescue:

```
df['Vote'].value_counts().to_frame()
Vote
Nay         263
Yea         56
```

Not a happy end, I'm afraid. The bill was shot down in flames.

Automating vote tabulation

That's how a single vote will look. Lets take what we've learned and build a program that will automate the process of scraping and then tabulating hundreds of votes at a time.

The first problem we'll need to solve is identifying the votes we want to analyse. I'll use our old friend `pd.read_html` to scrape the page that lists all the votes on private members' bills from the first session of the 42nd parliament. I'll then pass the data to a new dataframe called `vote_list`.

```
dfs_vote_list = pd.read_html('https://www.ourcommon\
s.ca/Members/en/votes?parlSession=42-1&billDocument\
TypeId=4',header=0)
vote_list = dfs_vote_list[0]
```

Now, since I'm going to have to keep track of the number of voting types as their records are scraped, I'll initialize some variables and set them to zero. There will be a party line and non party line variable for each party so we'll know how many of each category we've seen. I'll also track the total number of voting bills we're covering.

```
total_votes = 0
partyLineVotesConservative = 0
non_partyLineVotesConservative = 0
partyLineVotesLiberal = 0
non_partyLineVotesLiberal = 0
partyLineVotesNDP = 0
non_partyLineVotesNDP = 0
partyLineVotesBloc = 0
non_partyLineVotesBloc = 0
```

Once the core program is run, we'll iterate through four functions - one for each party. The functions will enumerate the Yeas and Nays and then test for the presence of at least one Yea and one Nay to identify split voting. If there was a split, the function will increment the non party line variable by one. Otherwise, the party line variable will be incremented by one.

Here's one of those functions:

```
def liberal_votes():
    global partyLineVotesLiberal
    global non_partyLineVotesLiberal

    df_party = df[df['Party'].str.contains('Liberal\
')]
    vote_output_yea = df_party['Vote'].str.contains\
('Yea')
    total_votes_yea = vote_output_yea.sum()
    vote_output_nay = df_party['Vote'].str.contains\
('Nay')
    total_votes_nay = vote_output_nay.sum()
    if total_votes_yea>0 and total_votes_nay>0:
```

```
        non_partyLineVotesLiberal += 1
    else:
        partyLineVotesLiberal += 1
```

Our next job will be to build a list of the URLs we'll be scraping. This example reads the private members' bills from the first session of the 42nd parliament. We're only interesting in collecting the relevant vote numbers from each row so we can add them to the base URL (identified as `https://www.ourcommons.ca/Members/en/votes/42/1/` in the code).

The problem is that the vote numbers are listed as `No. 1379` and so on. The string fragment `No.` is going to get in the way. The code `vote_list['Number'].str.extract('(\d+)', expand=False)` will strip out all non-numeric characters, leaving us with just the numbers themselves.

```
dfs_vote_list = pd.read_html('https://www.ourcommon\
s.ca/Members/en/votes?parlSession=42-1&billDocument\
TypeId=3',header=0)
vote_list = dfs_vote_list[0]
vote_list.columns = ['Number','Type','Subject','Vot\
es','Result','Date']
vote_list['Number'] = vote_list['Number'].str.extra\
ct('(\d+)', expand=False)
base_url = "https://www.ourcommons.ca/Members/en/vo\
tes/42/1/"
```

`url_data` is the name of a new dataframe I create to contain our set of production-ready URLs. I then run a for-loop that will iterate through each number from the `Number` column and add it to the end of the base URL. Each finished URL will then be appended to the `url_data` dataframe.

```
url_data = pd.DataFrame(columns=["Vote"])
Vote = []
for name in vote_list['Number']:
    newUrl = base_url + name
    Vote.append(newUrl)
url_data["Vote"] = Vote
```

The first lines of that dataframe will look like this:

```
url_data.head()
        Vote
0 https://www.ourcommons.ca/Members/en/votes/42/...
1 https://www.ourcommons.ca/Members/en/votes/42/...
2 https://www.ourcommons.ca/Members/en/votes/42/...
3 https://www.ourcommons.ca/Members/en/votes/42/...
4 https://www.ourcommons.ca/Members/en/votes/42/...
```

I'll want to save those URLs to a permanent file so they'll be available if I want to run similar queries later. Just be careful not to run this command more than once, as it will *add* a second (or third) identical set of URLs to the file, doubling (or tripling) the number of requests your program will make.

```
url_data.to_csv(r'url-text-42-1-privatemembers',
               header=None, index=None, sep=' ', m\
ode='a')
```

This brings us at last to the program's core. We'll use another for-loop to iterate through each URL in the file, read and convert the content to a dataframe, rename a couple of column headers to make them easier to work with, and then test for unanimous votes (i.e., bills which generated no Nay votes at all).

Why bother? Because unanimous votes - often motions to honour individuals or institutions - will teach us nothing about normal voting patterns and, on the contrary, could skew our results. If a vote was unanimous, `continue` will tell Python to skip it and move on to the next URL.

For all other votes (`else`), the code will call each of the four functions and then increment the `total_votes` variable by one.

```
URLS = open("url-text-42-1-privatemembers","r")
for url in URLS:
    # Read next HTML page in set:
    dfs = pd.read_html(url,header=0)
    df = dfs[0]
    df.rename(columns={'Member Voted':'Vote'}, inpl\
ace=True)
    df.rename(columns={'Political Affiliation':'Par\
ty'}, inplace=True)
    # Ignore unanimous votes:
    vote_output_nay = df[df['Vote'].str.contains('N\
ay', na=False)]
    total_votes_nay = vote_output_nay['Vote'].str.c\
ontains('Nay', na=False)
    filtered_votes = total_votes_nay.sum()
    if filtered_votes==0:
        continue
    # Call functions to tabulate votes:
    else:
        liberal_votes()
        conservative_votes()
        ndp_votes()
        bloc_votes()
```

```
        total_votes += 1
```

That's all the hard work. I wrapped things up by printing out each of the variables with their final values:

```
print("We counted", total_votes, "votes in total.")

print("Conservative members voted the party line", \
partyLineVotesConservative,
      "times, and split their vote", non_partyLineV\
otesConservative, "times.")
```

...And so on.

What did we learn?

Oh. You're still here? I guess you're curious about the results. Well how could I ever disappoint such a loyal and persistent reader? So here's what came back from scraping all government-sponsored bills from session 42-1:

```
We counted 424 votes in total.
Conservative members voted the party line 408 times\
, and split their vote 16 times.
Liberal members voted the party line 402 times, and\
 split their vote 22 times.
NDP members voted the party line 417 times, and spl\
it their vote 7 times.
Bloc members voted the party line 423 times, and sp\
lit their vote 1 times.
```

Out of 424 non-unanimous votes (there were 439 votes in total), Conservative members dissented from their party line 16 times, NDP members seven times, and the Bloc only once. But here's the interesting bit: Liberals - who, as I'm sure you know, were the government for this session - dissented more than any other group: 22 times. That's more than 5%. So much for my assumption about governing parties and party discipline. Or perhaps that's a product of the quality of their legislative program.

Party	Party-line votes	Non Party-line votes	Percentage
Conservative	408	16	96.23%
Liberal	402	22	94.81%
NDP	417	7	98.35%
Bloc	423	1	99.76%

Government Bills

The results did, however, confirm a separate assumption: split votes are, indeed, more common for private members' bills. Here's how those numbers looked:

Party	Party-line votes	Non Party-line votes	Percentage
Conservative	60	18	76.92%
Liberal	47	31	60.26%
NDP	74	4	94.87%
Bloc	76	2	97.44%

Private Members' Bills

I did wonder whether my 0-vote threshold for split votes was too strict. Perhaps having just one or two rogue members in a party vote isn't an indication of widespread independence. Would it be more accurate to set the cut off at a higher number, say 3? I can easily test this. All that's necessary is to change this line in each of the four party functions:

```
if total_votes_yea>0 and total_votes_nay>0:
```

To this:

```
if total_votes_yea>2 and total_votes_nay>2:
```

...And run the code again. When I did that, here's what came back:

Party	Party-line votes	Non Party-line votes	Percentage
Conservative	415	9	97.88%
Liberal	412	12	97.17%
NDP	423	1	99.76%
Bloc	423	1	99.76%

Government Bills (threshold = 3)

Party	Party-line votes	Non Party-line votes	Percentage
Conservative	66	12	84.62%
Liberal	57	21	73.08%
NDP	76	2	97.44%
Bloc	77	1	98.72%

Private Members' Bills (threshold = 3)

That's noticeably different, suggesting that there isn't *significant* voting dissension among the ranks of our political partics.

Could government be more representative?

When everything's said and done, our data showed that members for the most part voted with their parties *at least* 95% of the time. Given how they seem to vote, do we really need all those hundreds of MPs? Wouldn't it be enough to simply vote for a party and let whichever party wins select cabinet ministers from among all Canadian citizens?

Of course, MPs do much more than just vote. They work on parliamentary committees and attend to the needs of their constituents through local constituency offices.

But why couldn't parties appoint their own people to staff those committees? And why couldn't qualified individuals without official links to a political party be hired to staff constituency offices?

Ok. Now how about the fact that, behind the scenes, party caucuses provide important background and tone that helps party leaders formulate coherent and responsive policies? Yeah. Sure they do.

I'm not saying that MPs aren't, by and large, hard-working and serious public servants. And I don't think they're particularly overpaid. But I'm not sure how much grass roots-level representation they actually provide.

Does Wealth Influence the Prevalence of Mental Illness?

Having access to Python and Jupyter Notebook data analytics tools is empowering and, frankly, just plain fun. Ever argue with someone about a political or scientific subject and wish you could pull out a convincing argument that shuts the debate down? You know the kind I mean: "How come extreme weather events are happening so much more often than they used to?" I used to hear. "Actually," I can now cheerfully reply, "They're not." (See "Working With Major US Storm Data")

While learning more about the prevalence of various mental illnesses can't really be called "fun," it should at least be satisfying. And, considering how much excellent medical statistical data exists out there, it shouldn't be hard to get started.

What am I after here? We've always known that economic development has a measurable impact on health outcomes in general. The kinds of infrastructure that deliver clean water and well-supplied hospitals will cost a lot of money. But what about a connection between wealth and *mental* illnesses? Are people living in wealthy societies more or less likely to suffer from one or another form of mental illness? I've got some assumptions on that topic I'd like to test.

I have to pause here for a clear and emphatic

> disclaimer. I am not a mental health or medical professional. I have no training in either field and my opinions are therefore nothing more than opinions. Everything I'm going to say here in relation to mental health conditions should be understood in that context.
>
> Furthermore, regardless of what I'm going to say, the fact is that anyone suffering from a mental illness should seek professional guidance and therapy. These are very serious issues and my assumptions and speculation should never be used as a substitute for professional care - or as an attempt to minimize anyone's suffering.

The financial data I'm using here comes from the World Bank data.worldbank.org site[31] and presents per capita gross domestic product numbers from 2019.

```
import pandas as pd
import numpy as np
import matplotlib as plt
import matplotlib.pyplot as plt

gdp = pd.read_csv('WorldBank_PerCapita_GDP.csv')
gdp.head()
        Country         Value
0        Afghanistan         2156.4
1        Albania         14496.1
2        Algeria         12019.9
3        American Samoa          NaN
4        Andorra         NaN
```

[31]https://data.worldbank.org/indicator/NY.GDP.PCAP.PP.CD

The health data is from the GHD Results Tool on the Global Health Data Exchange site[32]. I used their drop-down configurations to select data by country that focused on the prevalence of individual illnesses measured as a rate per 100,000. These records also represent 2019.

After selecting just the two columns that interest me from each of the health CSV files ("Country" and "Val" - which is the average prevalence rate of the illness per 100,000 over the reporting period), here's what my data will look like:

```
anx = pd.read_csv('anxiety.csv')
anx = anx[['Country','Val']]
anx.head()
        Country         Val
0        Afghanistan         485.96
1        Albania        258.95
2        Algeria        817.41
3        American Samoa        73.16
4        Andorra        860.77
```

My assumptions

I'm only trying to measure prevalence, not outcomes or life expectancy. In that context, I would expect that medical conditions which seem related more to organic than environmental conditions should appear more or less evenly across societies at all stages of economic development. The prevalence of conditions that are more likely the result of environmental influences should, on the other hand, vary between economic strata.

[32]http://ghdx.healthdata.org/gbd-results-tool

Here's my untested theory: relative wealth, to some degree, frees people from many primary worries like finding their next meal and a safe place to sleep that night. As access to material benefits spreads, populations enjoy more leisure time, allowing individuals to spend only a finite number of a day's hours at work, and leaving the rest for personal pursuits.

Free time, as we all know, comes with its own costs. The lifestyle changes that result can introduce many unintended consequences, including those that impact our health and well being. To me it feels intuitive that the "anxiety disorders" category might include illness resulting from some "free time-induced" stresses.

Or, to put it a different way, people faced by immediate existential threats (like war or extreme poverty) would be less likely to notice or worry about many of the "first-world" concerns that make us anxious. This is certainly not to suggest that such suffering isn't real or important. But it would seem it should be unique to wealthier times and places. In addition, populations with less money and weaker access to mental health professionals are likely to see fewer positive diagnoses of anxiety disorders - even if the illness were present in equal numbers.

Conversely, I would expect incidents of schizophrenia to be more evenly distributed across all regions: after all what are the economic factors that could play a role, here? Aren't the primary risk factors for schizophrenia recreational drug use, childhood trauma, and genetics? These, unfortunately, would seem to be relatively uniform across all societies. And even if, like anxiety disorders, schizophrenia was under reported, the two effects would just cancel each other out when we compare them.

That's what I expected. Let's see what I actually got.

Plotting the data

After loading the libraries we'll need to generate a scatter plot, I'll merge my anxiety disorder data frame (anx) with the GDP data using pd.merge. I would do the same to merge my schrizophrenia data (sch).

```
import plotly.graph_objs as go
import plotly.express as px
merged_data_anx = pd.merge(gdp, anx, on='Country')
merged_data_anx = merged_data_anx[['Country', 'Valu\
e', 'Val']]
merged_data_anx.dropna(axis=0, how='any', thresh=No\
ne,
                   subset=None, inplace=True)
```

Plotting the graph won't involve anything we haven't seen before in these projects. The `labels` argument is used to make the plot more readable by assigning descriptive axis labels.

```
fig = px.scatter(merged_data_anx, x="Val", y="Value\
",
                 trendline="ols", log_x=True,
                 labels={
                     "Value": "GDP (in dollars)",
                     "Val": "Prevalence of Anxiety \
Disorders (/100k)"
                 },
                 hover_data=["Country", "Val"])
fig.show()
```

And here's what came out the other end:

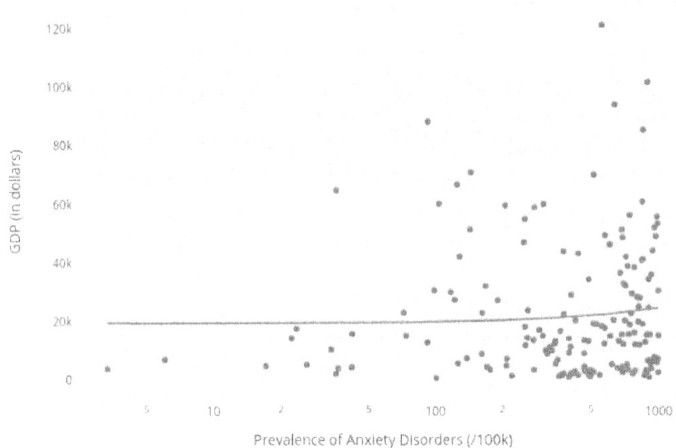

Whoops. That doesn't look anything like what I expected. As you can see, the regression line is nearly flat, indicating that there's very little variance in prevalence between rich and poor nations. In fact, there's quite a cluster of high-prevalence countries at the right edge of the X-axis along the very bottom (i.e., the least wealthy regions). If anything, anxiety disorders are *more* prevalent in countries with *lower* GDP.

Ok. So what about schizophrenia? Here's how that went:

```
fig = px.scatter(merged_data_sch, x="Val", y="Value\
",
                 trendline="ols", log_x=True,
                 labels={
                     "Value": "GDP (in dollars)",
                     "Val": "Prevalence of Schizoph\
renia (/100k)"
                 },
                 hover_data=["Country", "Val"])
fig.show()
```

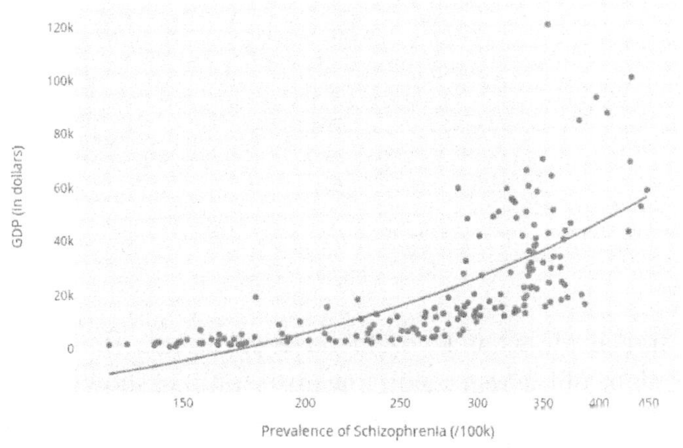

Another whoops. Here we're getting a significant *increase* in prevalence of schizophrenia as we move up the Y-axis towards higher GDP rates. The lowest rate among "developed" nations was Denmark, which reported a rather high 286 cases per 100,000.

So I'm 0 for 2. My intuition was clearly wrong.

To confirm all this, let's push that flawed intuition a bit further. I'll take a medical disease that should have - at best - minimal cultural connections. If there were even a shred of truth to my assumptions, we should see very little variation between countries. Well, using all the same code, here's how that turned out for pancreatic cancer:

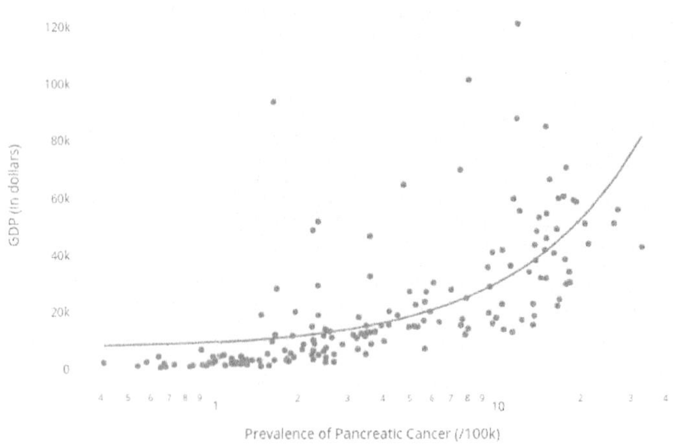

Again: not at all what I would have predicted. That clear upward slope of the regression line (or trendline) shows us an unmistakable correlation between higher wealth and higher incidents of pancreatic cancer. What's going on here?

Thinking about our data

The simple answer is that I have no clue what I'm doing. And as a general rule, that'll be a safe bet. But it would still be nice to have some sense of at least the outline of the problem.

So here are some thoughts.

Correlation, as I'm sure you've already heard, is not the same as causation. It's true that, for our schizophrenia plot, our regression line did seem to show a dependent variable (the prevalence of anxiety disorders we've been exploring) mapping rather neatly to an independent variable (the GDP indicator of wealth). But that doesn't prove that one actually *causes* the other.

There may be external variables impacting our numbers. Perhaps, for instance, the way people self-report their mental health will vary by culture. While epidemiological studies try to control for such differences, they're not perfect.

Or perhaps there's a relatively low level of stress that normal human beings can endure before common responses kick in. If that's true, then objective variations in stress levels (famine vs. workplace worries, for example) wouldn't matter much. Once the needle on the dial hits "red," anxiety happens.

That might explain how so many of the Holocaust survivors I knew in my youth were no less stable and productive than their peers who had grown up without suffering those years of unspeakable horror. Maybe, on some level, we just don't process stress above a certain limit

And when it comes to schizophrenia, perhaps the recreational drug use risk factor is mostly relevant to the more expensive drugs used in richer countries.

What about pancreatic cancer? Here there could be all kinds of environmental factors at play like diet and exercise. And the higher life expectancies of developed countries might just give such diseases more time to advance.

This last one is a possibility I can test. The R-squared value of the regression line I got when plotting pancreatic cancer rates across all ages was 0.418804. That would mean that 41.8% of my data points fit the expected correlation. Or, in other words, cancer rates rose in relatively close conformity with GDP.

But if I limited my data to cases at ages below 70, the R-squared number dropped to 0.371886, and further limiting it to a maximum of 54 years, saw another drop to 0.320124. At the other end, taking into account *only* people *above* the age of 70 gave us a much higher R-square of 0.543030. The chart below displays those values.

Age Range	R-Squared Value
70 and up	0.54303
All Ages	0.418804
Below 70	0.371886
Between 25-54	0.320124

What this shows is a clear progression: the lower the age under consideration, the less the impact a society's wealth has on prevalence of pancreatic cancer.

Do Birthdays Make Elite Athletes?

Do Birthdays Matter in Sports?

I'll begin with the question I'm going to try to answer: are you more likely to succeed as an elite athlete if your birthday happened to fall early in the calendar year?

It's been claimed that youth sports that divide participants by age and set the yearly cutoff at December 31 unwittingly make it harder for second-half-of-the-year players to succeed. That's because they'll be compared with players six to ten months older than them. At younger ages, those months can make a very big difference in physical strength, size, and coordination. If you were a minor league coach looking to invest in talent for a better team in a stronger league, who would you choose? And who would likely benefit more over the long term from your extra attention?

This is where the well-known writer, thinker, (and fellow Canadian) Malcolm Gladwell comes in. Gladwell wasn't actually the source of this insight (although he's the one most often associated with it). Rather, those honors fall to the psychologist Roger Barnesly who noticed an oddly distributed birthdate pattern among players at a junior hockey game he was attending. Why were so many of those talented athletes born early in the year? Gladwell just mentioned Barnesly's insight in his book, Outliers, which was where I came across it.

But is all that true? Was Barnesly's observation just an intriguing guess, or does real-world data bear him out?

Where Does the NHL Hide Its Data?

A couple of my kids are still teenagers so, for better or for worse, there's no escaping the long shadow of hockey fandom in my house. To feed their bottomless appetites for such things, I shared with them the existence of a robust official but undocumented API maintained by the National Hockey League. This URL:

```
https://statsapi.web.nhl.com/api/v1/teams/15/roster
```

...for instance, will produce a JSON-formatted dataset containing the official current roster of the Washington Capitals. Changing that `15` in the URL to, say, `10`, would give you the same information about the Toronto Maple Leafs.

There are many, many such endpoints as part of the API. Many of those endpoints can, in addition, be modified using URL expansion syntax.

> Fun fact: if you look at the site icon in the browser tab while on an NHL API-generated web page, you'll see the Major League Baseball trademark. How did that happen?

How to Use Python to Scrape NHL Statistics

Knowing all that, I could scrape the endpoint for each team's roster for each player's ID number, and then use those IDs to query each player's unique endpoint and read his birthdate. After selecting only those players who were born in Canada (after all, those are the only ones I know about whose cutoff was on December 31), I could then extract the birth month from each NHL player into a Pandas dataframe where the entire set could be computed and displayed as a histogram.

Here's the code I wrote to make all that happen. We begin, as always, by importing the libraries we'll need:

```
import pandas as pd
import requests
import json
import matplotlib.pyplot as plt
import numpy as np
```

Next, I'll create an empty dataframe (`df3`) that'll contain a column called `months`. I'll then use an `if` loop to read through all the team IDs between one and `11` (more on that later) and insert the value of each iteration of `team_id` into a "roster" endpoint address. The `.format(team_id)` code does that.

I'll then read the data from each endpoint page into the variable `r`, and read *that* into a dataframe called `roster_data`. Using `pd.json_normalize`, I'll read the contents of the `roster` section into a new dataframe, `df`.

I'll run *that* through a new nested `for` loop that'll apply `df.iterrows` that will add the birthdate data from each new roster page that the next lines of code will scrape. As we did before for teams, we'll insert each `person.id` record into the new endpoint and save it to the variable `url`. I'll then scrape the `birthDate` field for each player, read it to the `birthday` variable and, after first stripping unnecessary characters, read *that* to `newmonth`. Finally, I'll pull the `birthCountry` status from the page and, using `if`, drop the player if the value is anything *besides* `CAN`.

All that will then be plotted in a histogram using `df3.months.hist()`. Take a few minutes to look over this code to make sure it all makes sense.

```
df3 = pd.DataFrame(columns=['months'])
for team_id in range(1, 11, 1):
    url = 'https://statsapi.web.nhl.com/api/v1/team\
s/{}/roster'.format(team_id)
    r = requests.get(url)
    roster_data = r.json()
    df = pd.json_normalize(roster_data['roster'])
    for index, row in df.iterrows():
        newrow = row['person.id']
        url = 'https://statsapi.web.nhl.com/api/v1/\
people/{}'.format(newrow)
        newerdata = requests.get(url)
        player_stats = newerdata.json()
        birthday = (player_stats['people'][0]['birt\
hDate'])
        newmonth = int(birthday.split('-')[1])
        country = (player_stats['people'][0]['birth\
Country'])
        if country=='CAN':
            df3 = df3.append({'months': newmonth}, \
ignore_index=True)
```

```
        else:
            continue
df3.months.hist()
```

Before moving on, I should add a few notes:

- Be careful how and how often you use this code. There are nested for/loops that mean running the script even once will hit the NHL's API with more than a thousand queries. And that's assuming everything goes the way it should. If you make a mistake, you could end up annoying people you don't want to annoy.
- This code (`for team_id in range(1, 11, 1):`) actually only scrapes data from eleven teams. For some reason, certain API roster endpoints failed to respond to my queries and actually crashed the script. So, to get as much data as I could, I ran the script multiple times. This one was the first of those runs. If you want to try this yourself, remove the `df3 = pd.DataFrame(columns=['months'])` line from subsequent iterations so you don't inadvertently reset the value of your DataFrame to zero.
- Once you've successfully scraped your data, use something like `df3.to_csv('player_data.csv')` to copy your data to a CSV file, allowing you to further analyze the contents even if the original dataframe is lost. It's always good to avoid placing an unnecessary load on the API origin.

How to Visualize the Raw Data

Ok. Where was I? Right. I've got my data - the birth months of nearly 1,100 current NHL players - and I want to see what it looks like. Well wait no longer, here it is in all its glory:

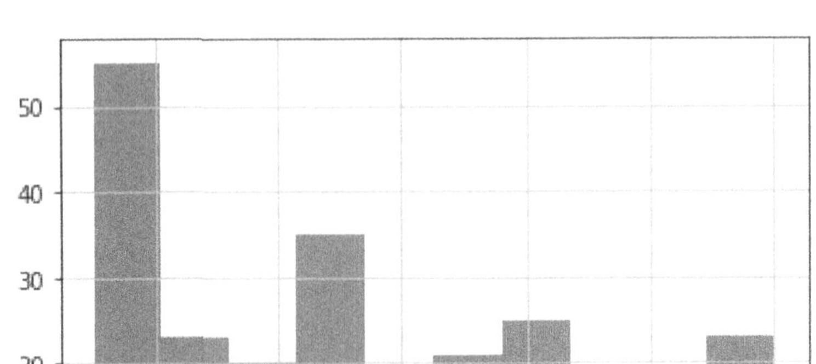

Historgram - the default version

What have we got here? Looks to me like January births do, indeed, account for a disproportionately high number of players but, then, so does December. And, overall, I just don't see the pattern that Gladwell's idea predicted. Aha! Shot down in flames. Never trust an intellectual!

Err. Not so fast there, youngster. Are we sure we're reading this histogram correctly? Remember: we're just starting out in this field and learning on the job. The default settings may not actually have given us what we thought they would. Note, for instance, how we're measuring the frequency of births over 12 months, but there are only ten bars in the chart!

What's going on here?

What Do Histograms Really Tell Us?

Let's look at the actual numbers behind this histogram. You can get those numbers by loading the CSV file you might have earlier exported using `df3.to_csv('player_data.csv')`. Here's how you might go about getting that done:

```
import pandas as pd
df = pd.read_csv('player_data.csv')
df['months'].value_counts()
```

And here's what my output looked like (I added the column headers manually):

```
Month Frequecy
5     35
2     29
1     26
8     25
3     23
7     21
4     20
6     18
10    17
12    13
11    10
9     10
```

Looks like there were nearly double the births the first four months of the year than in the final four. Now that's *exactly* what Gladwell's prediction would expect. So then what's up with the histogram?

Let's run it again, but this time, I'll specify 12 bins rather than the default ten.

```
import pandas as pd
df = pd.read_csv('player_data.csv')
df.hist(column='months', bins=12);
```

A "bin" is actually an approximation of a statistically appropriate interval between sets of your data. Bins attempt to guess at the *probability density function (PDF)* that will best represent the values you're actually using. But they may not display exactly the way you'd think - especially when you use the default value. Here's what we're shown using 12 bins:

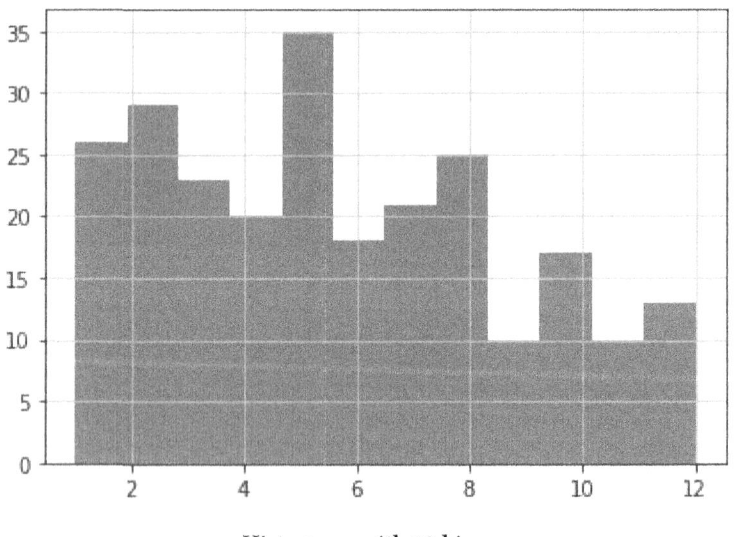

Histogram with 12 bins

This one probably shows us an accurate representation of our data the way we'd expect to see it. I say "probably," because there could be some idiosyncrasies with the way histograms divide their bins I'm not aware of.

Make Sure to Use the Right Tools For the Job

But it turns out that the humble histogram was actually the wrong visualization tool for our needs.

Histograms are great for showing frequency distributions by grouping data points together into bins. This can help us quickly visualize the state of a very large dataset where granular precision will get in the way. But it can be misleading for use-cases like ours.

Instead, let's go with a plain old bar graph that incorporates our `value_counts` numbers. I'll pipe the results of `value_counts` to a dataframe called `df2` and then plot that as a simple bar graph.

```
df2 = df['months'].value_counts()
df2.plot(kind='bar')
```

Running that will give us something a bit easier to read that's also more intuitively reliable:

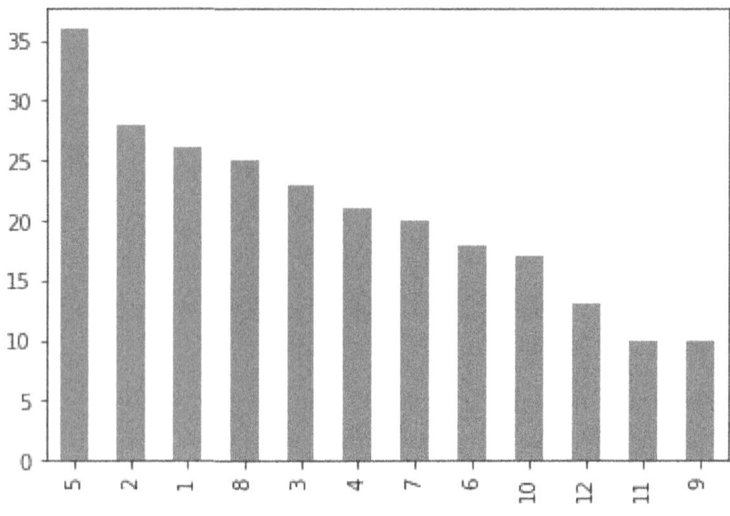

Bar plot: much easier to read

That's better, no? We can see the months (represented by numbers) displayed in order of highest births with five of the top six months occurring between January and May.

The moral of the story? Data is good. Histograms are good. But it's also good to know how to read them and when to use them.

Do Gun Control Laws Impact Gun Violence?

Gun control laws regularly inspire heated debate, although rarely useful insight.

All decent people agree that eliminating violent crimes should be prominent on every agenda. The trick is in deciding what's the best way to get there. Some argue that limiting a population's access to lethal weapons is the most direct way to prevent their misuse. Others, arguing with similar passion, insist that no law will stop criminals from finding the weapons they're after, but their potential victims should be allowed the means to defend themselves (as they say: "When seconds count, the police are only minutes away").

This article has no opinion on all that. But it is curious to know if there's any statistical evidence supporting the *effectiveness* of gun control laws. In other words, do jurisdictions with strong laws consistently experience lower rates of gun violence? It would seem that any clear correlation between legislation and violence should help inform intelligent public policy.

As you might expect, there are many useful data resources we can draw on. In the interests of keeping things simple, we'll stick to just a few easy-to-access data sets - and just one or two data points from each of those. Specifically, we're going to explore the relationship between concealed carry laws and gun deaths through homicide. Personal injuries, financial crimes, and suicides committed with the use of a gun, while tragic, will not be our focus.

For practical reasons we'll also need to distinguish between the United States and the rest of the world. The problem with the US is that, according to federal law, concealed carry is perfectly legal, but many individual states impose their own licensing requirements. Practically, this makes citizens' access to guns in the US highly dependent on their particular state. For that reason, there's no value in comparing overall US statistics with the rest of the world. Instead, we'll rank US states separately.

Quantifying International Gun Laws

Finding a way to define gun control legislation that'll make sense across the widest range of countries isn't going to be easy. Take a look through the information on the Wikipedia "Overview of gun laws by nation" page[33] to get a sense of the problem. You'll quickly see that finding a single legal standard that's universally common isn't possible. Some nations distinguish between weapon types or uses that others lump together. Often, it's not a simple matter of "legal" or "illegal," but licencing rules that are conditional on multiple factors.

The most useful proxy I can find is "concealed carry." And I'll use the table from that Wikipedia page. The table may look intimidating from the perspective of importing its data into Python, but there's a great online website called wikitable2csv.ggor.de[34] that will do all the world for us. We just

[33]https://en.wikipedia.org/wiki/Overview_of_gun_laws_by_nation
[34]https://wikitable2csv.ggor.de/

need to paste the Wikipedia URL, click Convert, and the site does all the rest.

With that, we're ready to begin. After importing the libraries we'll need, we can read our new CSV file into a data frame.

```
import pandas as pd
import matplotlib as plt
import matplotlib.pyplot as plt

# https://en.wikipedia.org/wiki/Overview_of_gun_law\
s_by_nation
df = pd.read_csv('wikipedia_gun_law_table.csv')
```

The first thing I'll do is update the name of the concealed carry column. Currently it's `Concealed carry[8]` which will unnecessarily complicate things. Just plain old `Carry` will work fine:

```
df.rename(columns={'Concealed carry[8]':'Carry'}, i\
nplace=True)
```

I'll then get rid of the ten columns we won't be using by reading just the country column `Region` and `Carry` into our data frame:

```
df = df[['Region', 'Carry']]
df.head()
        Region                         Carry
0         Afghanistan[9][law 1] Restricted
1         Albania[law 2] Self-defense permits
2         Algeria[10] No[N 2]
3         Andorra[law 3] Justification required
4         Angola[11] Restricted
```

This gives us a good view of some issues. Those brackets hold footnotes which, while important, are only going to get in our way. Besides brackets, the `Carry` column also has parentheses. These three commands will get rid of those markings and all the text they enclose:

```
df['Region'] = df['Region'].str.replace(r"\[.*\]","\
")
df['Carry'] = df['Carry'].str.replace(r"\[.*\]","")
df['Carry'] = df['Carry'].str.replace(r"\(.*\)","")
```

Now everything we want to do here depends on the values in the `Carry` column. The problem here, as the screenshot of the output of the `value_counts()` command shows us, is that there are nearly 30 unique values - many of them overlapping. It'll be hard to track trends when there's so little uniformity between legal standards.

```
df['Carry'].value_counts().to_frame()
```

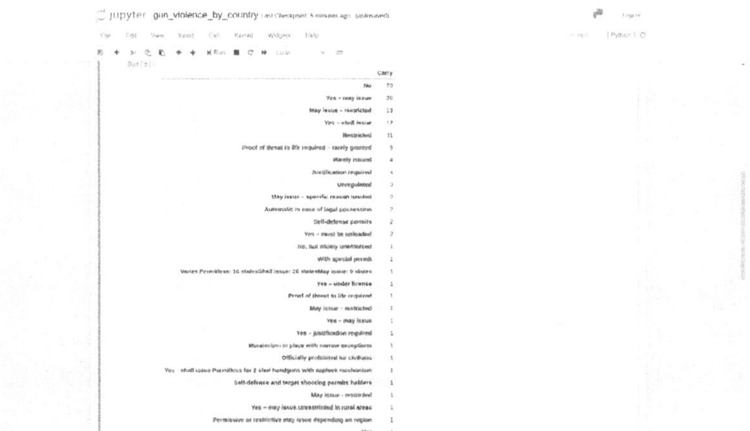

Output of the value_counts() command

So, wherever possible, I'll try to combine multiple values where they're intuitively similar. As it turns out, for instance, any row that contained the word `Yes` or `No` does indeed at least largely match the intent of a straight `Yes` (i.e., concealed carry is permitted) or `No` (i.e., it's prohibited). This will bring the list of unique values down to about 18. Better.

```
import re
df['Carry'].replace(re.compile('.*Yes.*'), 'Yes', i\
nplace=True)
df['Carry'].replace(re.compile('.*Rarely.*'), 'Rare\
ly', inplace=True)
df['Carry'].replace(re.compile('.*rarely.*'), 'Rare\
ly', inplace=True)
df['Carry'].replace(re.compile('.*No.*'), 'No', inp\
lace=True)
df['Carry'].replace(re.compile('.*Restrict.*'), 'Re\
strict', inplace=True)
df['Carry'].replace(re.compile('.*restrict.*'), 'Re\
strict', inplace=True)
```

But not good enough yet. If you run `value_counts()` once again, you'll see that there are quite a few values that apply to only one or two countries. Since those won't be statistically significant, we can dump them. I'll choose a unique string from each of those and use it to remove their rows:

```
df = df[~df.Carry.str.contains("Justification", na=\
False)]
df = df[~df.Carry.str.contains("legal", na=False)]
df = df[~df.Carry.str.contains("states", na=False)]
df = df[~df.Carry.str.contains("Moratorium", na=Fal\
se)]
df = df[~df.Carry.str.contains("specific", na=False\
)]
```

Whatever's left after all that won't cause us any trouble.

Importing Gun Violence Data

We're now ready for our gun violence data. For this, we'll use numbers from the World Population Review site[35]. Their "Gun Deaths by Country 2021" table contains four values for each country: *Firearm-related death rate per 100,000 population per year, Homicide rate per year, Suicide rate per year*, and *Total death number per year.* We'll only be interested in the homicide rate column, but clicking the link to download CSV or JSON versions will get us the whole thing.

```
dfv = pd.read_csv('Gun-Related-Deaths_WPR.csv')
```

[35]https://worldpopulationreview.com/country-rankings/gun-deaths-by-country

To make it possible to integrate our two data frames, I'll rename the `country` column `Region` and, for clarity, `homicide` as `Homicides`. I'll then save just the two columns we want into a new data frame.

```
dfv.rename(columns={'country':'Region'}, inplace=Tr\
ue)
dfv.rename(columns={'homicide':'Homicides'}, inplac\
e=True)
dfv_data = dfv[['Region','Homicides']]
```

Plotting International Gun Violence Data

We should now be ready to merge our two data frames using `pd.merge`. `on='Region'` tells Pandas that the `Region` column in each source data frame should be the common reference.

```
merged_data = pd.merge(dfv_data, df, on='Region')
```

Here's what our new data frame will look like:

```
merged_data.head()
        Region         Homicides          Carry
0        El Salvador         26.49          Yes
1        Jamaica       30.38          Yes
2        Panama                14.36          Yes
3        Uruguay       4.78           Yes
4        Montenegro       2.42           Yes
```

Everything is now ready for us to generate a scatter plot that'll hopefully show us something useful. If you haven't already, install the Plotly library on your machine using `pip`.

```
$ pip install plotly
```

Now we can import the libraries into our Jupyter notebook:

```
import plotly.graph_objs as go
import plotly.express as px
```

And this code will build us a scatter plot, complete with the information that'll appear when we hover the mouse over a dot:

```
fig = px.scatter(merged_data, x="Homicides", y="Car\
ry", log_x=True,
                 hover_data=["Homicides", "Carry", \
"Region"])
fig.show()
```

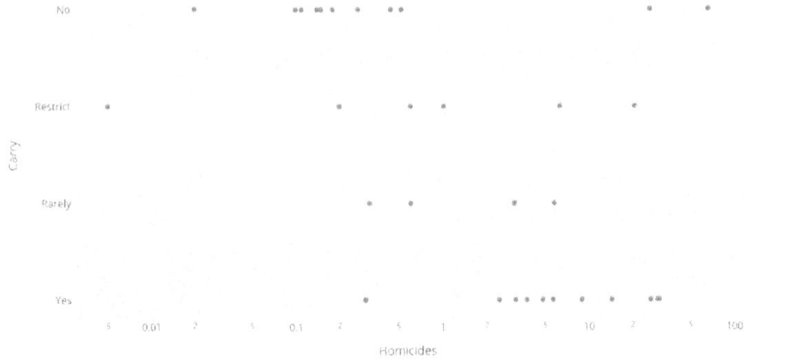

Note how Plotly spaced our homicide data across the X-axis. Because of the numbers we're getting, the check points (0.01, 0.1, 1, etc.) don't increase at a fixed rate, but by increments of ten. You can see that in action by hovering over the "No" point at the top right. Honduras, unfortunately, had more than 66 homicides for every 100,000 people in that year.

Scatter plot with a hover point visible

By contrast, Singapore had a microscopic murder rate of 0.005. To properly display a data set with such extremes, irregular spacing is necessary. Fortunately, Plotly does that for us automatically.

Ok. So what does it all tell us? First off, The `Restrict` and `Rarely` categories represent nations whose governments may permit conceal carry, but where it's unusual. If we were to group those together with the `No` category, then a quick visual scan of the plot would suggest roughly equivalent outcomes between legal standards.

I have no idea if this has any significance but, except for Philippines, every single country whose gun murder rate is higher than 1/100,000 is in South or Central America or the Caribbean. What *is* significant is that those 17 countries are more or less evenly split between permissive and (largely) prohibitive gun carry legislation - and two of the top five rates are from “No” jurisdictions. The actual numbers are seven “No” and ten “Yes.”

On the other end of the spectrum, countries with very low murder rates skew heavily (14 to 1) towards restrictive laws.

On the other hand, suppose we were to group `Restrict` together with `Yes`. Perhaps “restrict” makes more sense as “yes, but with some restrictions.” In that case, the top 17 would be shifted to 13 (Yes) to 4 (No). But the bottom 15 would now be a bit more evenly balanced: 11 to 4.

Are more conclusive conclusions possible? Perhaps we need more data, or a better way to interpret and “translate” legal standards. But, either way, let’s turn our attention to data covering US states.

US Gun Laws and Gun Violence

I used a separate Jupyter notebook for this process. If you decide to stick both the world and US data together, be sure to update the data frame naming accordingly.

I’ll begin with data downloaded from the World Population Review *Gun Laws by State 2021* page[36]. I’ll load the CSV file in as always using Pandas:

```
df = pd.read_csv('US-carry-laws-by-state-WPR.csv')
```

For clarity, I’ll rename the `permitReqToCarry` column as `PermitRequired` and rewrite the data frame with only that and the State columns:

[36]https://worldpopulationreview.com/state-rankings/gun-laws-by-state

```
df.rename(columns={'permitReqToCarry':'PermitRequir\
ed'}, inplace=True)
df = df[['State','PermitRequired']]
```

As you can see from the Wyoming record in this `head` output, the table represents a negative value (i.e., no permit is required) as `NaN`. to make things easier for us, I'll use `fillna` to replace those values with `False`.

```
df.head(10)
        State                 PermitRequired
0        Washington         True
1        New York         True
2        New Jersey         True
3        Michigan         True
4        Maryland         True
5        Hawaii                 True
6        Connecticut         True
7        California         True
8        Wyoming         NaN
9        Wisconsin         True
```

```
df.PermitRequired.fillna('False', inplace=True)
```

That'll be all we'll need for the legal side. I'll use data from another Wikipedia page[37] to provide us with information about gun violence. I manually removed the columns we're not interested in before importing the CSV file.

[37]https://en.wikipedia.org/wiki/Gun_violence_in_the_United_States_by_state

```
dfv = pd.read_csv('gun_violence_by_US_State_Wikiped\
ia.csv')
```

Running head against the data frame shows us we've got some cleaning up to do: there isn't data for every state (as you can see from Alabama). So I'll run `str.contains` to remove those rows altogether.

```
dfv.head()
        State                    GunMurderRate
0         Alabama           â€”  [a]
1         Alaska                      5.3
2         Arizona           2.5
3         Arkansas           3.7
4         California           3.3
```

```
dfv = dfv[~dfv.GunMurderRate.str.contains("]", na=F\
alse)]
```

Just as we did with the world data earlier, I'll create a `merged_data` data frame, this time referenced on the `State` column.

```
merged_data = pd.merge(dfv, df, on='State')
```

Once again - making sure Plotly is properly imported - I'll plot my data:

```
import plotly.graph_objs as go
import plotly.express as px

fig = px.scatter(merged_data, x="GunMurderRate", y=\
"PermitRequired",
                 log_x=True,
                 hover_data=["GunMurderRate", "Perm\
itRequired", "State"])
fig.show()
```

And here's what that gives us:

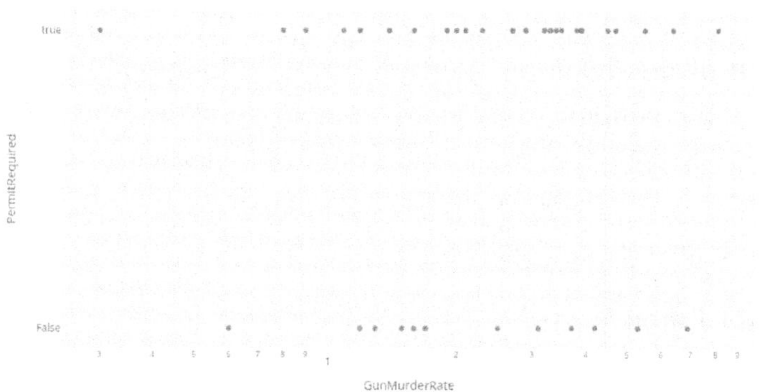

Not very pretty, but it does give us a quick view of the action. The most noticeable feature is that there are far more states that require permits ("true") than that don't ("false"). Having said that, the "permit" states seem, on the whole, to be more clustered towards the dangerous end of the plot, led by Louisiana at 8.1 murders per 100,000 people.

The good news is that no US state has a murder rate that would rank anywhere near the "top" 17 countries we saw earlier. The better news, at least for those who live in Hawaii, is that citizens of that state enjoy great weather *and* a gun murder rate of 0.3. Not quite Singapore territory, but not bad at all.

But I think it's reasonable to conclude from the US data at least, that stronger gun laws do *not* seem to have a noticeable effect on reducing gun crimes.

What's next?

Well that's entirely up to you. As for me, I wish you great success as you now embark on your own data journey.

There is one thing I would request of you. Writing an honest review of this book on Amazon can go a long way to help expose the content to as many eyes as possible. And being able to see your insights would also make it easier for people to assess whether the book is a good match for their needs.

Either way, be in touch,

David Clinton[38]

The Data Project[39]

[38]https://bootstrap-it.com/davidclinton/
[39]https://thedataproject.net

Made in the USA
Monee, IL
11 July 2021